#because2020

Mike Lauterborn

authorHOUSE®

AuthorHouse™
1663 Liberty Drive
Bloomington, IN 47403
www.authorhouse.com
Phone: 833-262-8899

Published by AuthorHouse 03/19/2021

ISBN: 978-1-6655-1949-6 (sc)
ISBN: 978-1-6655-1948-9 (e)

Library of Congress Control Number: 2021904996

Print information available on the last page.

Preface

Record-breaking weather events. Strange beasties that literally created a buzz. A restless universe tossing rocks at our planet. All with a raging coronavirus afflicting our world population. Just some of the bizarre happenings that defined 2020. Captured in one bucket here, the read is dizzying and dramatic… and worrying with regard to the future. Are these splashes a glimpse of more aggressive and violent weather, nature and space occurrences to come?

Friday, January 29, 2021

Red, mocking mercury glaring 12F here along the shore in Fairfield, CT. A "feels like" temp of -6F due to 25 mph persistent, face-shearing winds from the northwest, rushing down from Ontario across Michigan's forehead, hugging the choppy surfaces of Lake Huron and Lake Erie, and driving through the grooves of western New York and into our back yards, rattling our houses and raking our trees, causing limbs to rip away and take down electric wires before crashing to the ground. Online power maps lighting up with unplanned outage reports, zip codes affected, restoration estimates and repair crew status. The National Weather Service issuing a Warning about Winter Storm Orlena for the Metro New York area, with a forecast of a massive system expected to bring 12-22 inches of snow, wind gusting to 50 mph, blizzard conditions, coastal flooding, and beach erosion to the region over the next few days.

These alarming conditions and urgent alerts seemed the appropriate background to reflect on 2020, specific to weather, strange beasts across our planet, and the record-setting, often ferocious, sometimes once-in-a-lifetime occurrences that took place both on our Earth and in the heavens. Our planet was restless and her tantrums seemed to be getting worse, pointing to inevitable changes in climate, sea rise, fresh water availability and food production. Combined with the impact of a near-invisible Covid-19 virus that had, to date, impacted over 100 million people and resulted in over 2.2 million deaths worldwide, along with political unrest and sharp division of people and ideologies here in the United States and many other parts of the globe, the future appeared bleak. The following offers a detailed log of the events in those categories that rose to the top as most notable or impactful…

Tumbleweeds, Wildfires & Quakes

January 1, 2020

"Tumbleweed Causes Trouble", noted ListVerse, as a first entry to 2020. Certainly a curious, must-know-more-invoking headline. "As the hours ticked by on New Year's Eve 2019, some drivers near Yakima, Washington, saw in the new year trapped on a highway," the list-making website began. Specifically, "A massive wall of tumbleweed left them stranded in their vehicles for about 10 hours while workers tried to uncover cars that had been completely buried beneath the invader plants. Two snowplows were used to clear the tumbleweeds after they were blown onto State Highway 240 during strong winds." A state policeman onsite, Chris Thorson, remarked that, in twenty years on the job, he had never seen anything quite like the sight of the giant tumbleweeds blocking cars. ListVerse added that tumbleweed is usually linked to the American West but originated in the Ural Mountain steppe in Russia. Nowadays it could be found all over the world, including Afghanistan and even New Zealand.

While these tumbleweeds were tying up traffic, AccuWeather was forecasting a "Winter storm train to hammer the northwestern U.S. well into January 2020". Not the weather report you prefer to hear as you kick off a new 365-day cycle. "Unrelenting storms will escalate the risk of flash flooding, mudslides and avalanches as ski resorts continue to be bombarded with heavy snow," the weather reporting resource said. One of their senior meteorologists, Brian Thompson, added, "Expect rounds of strong winds from the storms with the potential for power outages."

The main thrust of the storms, AccuWeather said, was going to focus on British Columbia and western Washington. "A general 3-6 inches of rain will fall, but … 12 inches is likely on the west-facing slopes of the Olympic, Cascade and Coast Mountains," it shared. Worse: "The cumulative effect of each storm will make the hillsides unstable. With each round of drenching rain, the risk of mudslides and other debris flows will increase over the lower elevations. Episodes of heavy rain in low and intermediate elevations will cause streams and rivers to run high with the risk of flooding." And while that rain was dropping and having its effect, the passes over the high country were going to get whomped with "a heavy load of snow, on the order of 3-6 feet with local amounts to 9 feet" piling up over the next week. Further: "The snow load from each storm and periodic gusty winds can make the snowpack unstable with an increasing risk of avalanches."

Hello 2020.

January 2

On the other side of the world, The Diplomat reported "30 Dead, Thousands Caught in Flooding in Indonesia's Capital". Jakarta had been socked by widespread floods which drove a death toll up to 30 "with thousands more displaced as waters began to recede." The paper cited that "monsoon rains and rising rivers submerged at least 182 neighborhoods in greater Jakarta… and caused landslides in the Bogor and Depok districts on the city's outskirts."

Officials initially said 35,000 people were in shelters across the greater metropolitan area and that "those returning to their homes found streets covered in mud and debris. Cars that had been parked in driveways were swept away, landing upside down in parks or piled up in narrow alleys. Sidewalks were strewn with sandals, pots, pans and old photographs."

Flood waters reached more than eight feet in some places. Even the runways at the capital's airport were submerged. The incident qualified as the worst flooding since 2013, when 47 people were killed after Jakarta was inundated by monsoon rains.

In Jakarta's satellite cities of Bekasi and Tangerang, where rivers had burst their banks, large areas remained inundated, according to The Diplomat. "Residents of Bekasi waded through water up to their necks or floated on makeshift rafts carrying clothes and other salvaged possessions.

Some scrambled onto roofs to await rescue from soldiers and emergency workers in rubber dinghies."

Social affairs minister Juliari Peter Batubara confirmed that the government dispatched medical teams and rubber rafts to the worst-hit areas, while rescuers in boats delivered instant noodles and rice to those who chose to stay on the upper floors of their homes, according to the paper.

January 5

Winter Storm Henry defined the wintry activity AccuWeather had forecast. While those pesky tumbleweeds were bothering Washington state, Henry was impacting the region to the east, The Weather Channel detailed. The storm "spread rain and high-elevation snow into the Pacific Northwest on Dec. 31, then brought heavier snow to parts of the Intermountain West on New Year's Day. Parts of Idaho, western Montana, Wyoming, western Colorado and northern Utah picked up snow through late on New Year's Day, including Salt Lake City where enough snow was expected to issue winter storm warnings… More than a foot of snow fell in Utah's Wasatch, including in Alta, Utah, which picked up 16 inches."

The highest snowfall totals from Henry were in southern Wyoming to the west of the Interstate 25 corridor, The Weather Channel continued. "Two to four feet of snow fell from Whiskey Park to Sugar Loaf, Wyoming. Winds gusted to near 60 mph along the Interstate 25 corridor on New Year's Day."

The storm apparently caused two deaths in western Montana. "Heavy, wet snow and gusty winds increased the instability of the new snowpack near Missoula, Montana, on New Year's Day, where three snowmobilers were hit by the avalanche. Two of the three were killed," TWC stated.

The storm flurried out over the Rockies on Jan. 2nd as it began to interact with a larger trough of low pressure over the country's heartland. "A few strong to severe storms rumbled across the South that day as a secondary low pressure system moved from coastal Texas to northern Alabama. Areas of flooding dotted cities from Jackson, Mississippi, to Nashville, Tennessee. Over 4 inches of rain flooded streets and parking lots and stranded vehicles in Jackson, Mississippi," said TWC. January 2 became Jackson's second wettest January day on record, picking up almost a month's worth of precipitation.

This low pressure system continued its roll. "The Holmes Lake Dam, a small dam in southern Hinds County, Mississippi, failed the night of Jan. 2, damaging a barn, several vehicles and a fence, according to local emergency management," said TWC. "In Natchez, Mississippi, at least five mudslides were reported along Martin Luther King Street. Flooding was also reported throughout Lowndes County, in northeast Mississippi, prompting closures of at least three roads."

In Falkville, Alabama, two adults and two children had to be rescued from a flooded vehicle on Jan. 3. Heavy rain continued across much of the South and East on Jan. 3, but flood concerns eased as the intensity of rainfall dropped. To the west, a small low pressure system produced snowfall in portions of Iowa and southern Minnesota, where up to nine inches of snow was dropped in northern Iowa. The energy from this low pressure system swirled eastward into the Ohio River Valley on Jan. 4, where it amplified snow flurries from Ohio to as far south as northern Georgia.

Henry finished up by bringing a few inches of snow to parts of northern New England Jan. 4 into early Jan. 5, concluded TWC.

In complete contrast, the opposite side of the globe was having one of its driest times ever. The Guardian announced "Australian heatwave: Canberra and Penrith smash temperature records that stood for 80 years". Located west of Sydney, Penrith hit 120F; Canberra hit 111F. Penrith's mark made it one of the hottest places in the world for the day, according to TG.

January 7

There was more "fun" on tap for the southern half of the United States. ABC News reported a quick-moving storm "moving east with severe weather and heavy snow for the South", including strong thunderstorms in eastern Texas and a possible tornado near Galveston. Damaging winds and large hail were also possible, ABC said.

ABC projected potential severe weather for Florida, too, and heavy snow for north Georgia, the Carolinas, East Tennessee and Southern

Virginia. A winter storm warning was issued from Georgia to Virginia, and some areas with high elevation in North Carolina were expected to get nine inches of snow.

January 8

We got our own winter whip-up here in the Northeast. The NWS New York NY issued a "Snow Squall Warning for the New York Tri-State Area. Hazard: White out conditions and heavy blowing snow. Impact: Dangerous life-threatening travel."

As the system moved through, Fairfield, CT's Fairfield HamletHub mused on its Facebook page late afternoon, "Such a strange weather day today in southwestern CT! First a snow squall then sun and now snow again with gusty wind and plunging temps as bands of winter weather move through the region."

Again, Down Under, the weather continued to get drier and more dangerous. The Guardian headlined: "Three Australian states face more dangerous bushfire weather".

TG said that firefighters and residents in southeastern Australia were bracing for the return of dangerous weather conditions. The country's bushfire crisis, which began in late 2019, had already burned through over 20.7 million acres, destroyed thousands of homes and killed at least 26 people, including three volunteer firefighters.

After a brief spell of mild weather, conditions were expected to worsen in parts of New South Wales, Victoria and South Australia, with temps around 104F and unpredictable winds set to sweep through a range of fire zones.

January 11-12

In a total wacky winter flip-flop, Weather.com shared "Boston Reaches the 70s in January During a Meeting of Meteorologists". Indeed, the mercury in Boston soared into the 70s two days in a row on the weekend of Jan. 11-12, during what would typically be the coldest time of the year, destroying the city's all-time January record on the 12th, at a balmy 74F.

Until this record-smasher, "Beantown" temps had reached 70F in January just twice, in 1876 and 1950. Normally, its average high this period is only 36F, Weather noted.

Adding a cake topper, the 100th annual meeting of the American Meteorological Society just happened to be kicking off this particular weekend in Boston. So, instead of typical wintry mush, meteorologists and scientists enjoyed unusual warmth for their gathering.

January 13

The Philippines was feeling the heat, too, but not in a pleasant way. NPR noted "Volcanic Eruption In Philippines Causes Thousands To Flee", reporting that a volcano south of the country's capital had "sent a massive plume of ash and steam spewing miles into the sky and pushed red-hot lava out of its crater, prompting the evacuation of thousands of people and the closure of Manila's airport."

In a matter of hours, the local seismic monitoring group, the Philippine Institute of Volcanology and Seismology, raised the alert level for the volcano in question, Taal, from Level 1 to 4, with Level 5 being the highest. It warned that a larger "explosive eruption" could occur within hours or days. The National Disaster Risk Reduction Management Council, the Philippines' disaster-response agency, said 13,000 villagers were moved away from the area to evacuation centers in Batangas and Cavite provinces. It told NPR that nearly 25,000 people had been displaced by the eruption. Others refused to leave their homes and farms, or could not leave because of a lack of transportation or poor visibility from the thick ash.

"Our people are panicking due to the volcano because they want to save their livelihood, their pigs and herds of cows," Mayor Wilson Maralit of Balete town told a local radio station. "We're trying to stop them from returning and warning that the volcano can explode again any time and hit them."

The Volcanology Institute cautioned that fine ash fall could cause breathing problems, especially among young children and the elderly, and advised the public in affected areas to use face masks or wet towels to protect themselves. It also advised motorists that the ash could reduce visibility and make roads slippery, according to NPR.

In Manila, long lines formed at shops selling face masks, with many residents likely remembering the 1991 eruption of Mount Pinatubo, about 55 miles northwest of the capital, which killed more than 350 people and blanketed the area in thick ash for miles around.

January 14

As ash rained down in the Philippines, The Guardian shared, "More than 130 dead as avalanches and floods hit Pakistan and Afghanistan". TG detailed, "Avalanches, flooding and harsh winter weather have killed more than 130 people across Pakistan and Afghanistan and left others stranded by heavy snowfall." TG added that at least 93 people died and 76 were injured across Pakistan in recent days – with several still missing – while a further 39 were killed in Afghanistan, according to officials. Pakistani Kashmir was apparently the worst-hit area, with 62 people killed and 10 others missing, the state disaster management authority stated. Forecasters suggested more harsh weather was on the way.

January 15

The southern U.S. had jumped into the lead car on a weather roller coaster, the ever-watchful Guardian said. "Devastating storms with embedded tornadoes swept across parts of the U.S., stretching over 600 miles from southeast Texas to Missouri at one point," it reported. "Heavy rain, strong winds and violent tornadoes resulted in widespread destruction and loss of life, with 11 deaths reported and more than 350,000 homes left without power. Cars were overturned and mobile homes were demolished, hundreds of flights were cancelled, and an estimated 5 million people were placed on a flood watch as the storms ripped through metropolitan areas."

And while the South was getting whipped, Australia continued to burn, with impacts there starting to affect the world, as Weather.com noted: "Australian Wildfire Smoke Circles the Globe". By this point, the catastrophic bushfires, sparked in 2019, had charred more than 20% of the country's forests, destroyed over 1,400 homes, and killed an estimated 1 billion animals, Weather said. Carried by wind currents, resulting smoke first arrived in South America (7,500 miles away), producing hazy skies in Santiago, Chile, and Buenos Aires, Argentina. The smoke ultimately toured the globe circling back to the area just south of Australia.

January 17

Winter popped its head up again here in southwestern Connecticut. The National Weather Service issued a Winter Weather Advisory in effect from 10am Sat. Jan. 18 to 1am Sun. Jan. 19, forecasting snow in the range of 2-4 inches, and told us to plan on slippery road conditions that could impact travel initially. It was more or less par for the winter course for us, but an alert nevertheless that we needed to heed.

Not *at all* par for the course, in Maryland, a high school student, just days into a NASA internship, discovered a distant exoplanet that orbits two stars, one of just a dozen such worlds known to scientists.

Wolf Cukier actually made his discovery during the Summer 2019, while at NASA's Goddard Space Flight Center in Maryland, after wrapping up his junior year at Scarsdale High School in Westchester, New York, but Space.com had only just gotten hold of the story and shared it.

"I was looking through the data for everything the volunteers had flagged as an eclipsing binary, a system where two stars circle around each other and, from our view, eclipse each other every orbit," Cukier said. "About three days into my internship, I saw a signal from a system called TOI 1338 b. At first I thought it was a stellar eclipse, but the timing was wrong. It turned out to be a planet."

The new addition to the exoplanet family was a gas planet about the size of Saturn, noted Space.com. The two stars it orbits are about 1,300 light-years away from our sun in the constellation Pictor. The data that Cukier looked at came from NASA's Transiting Exoplanet Survey Satellite (TESS). This exoplanet was TESS' first capture of a world that orbits two stars.

January 18

"Snowmageddon" was the word of the day, related to a massive winter blizzard in Newfoundland "that buried cars and left thousands without power," according to The Guardian.

TG said Canada's federal government would be helping the country dig itself out from a storm that dumped as much as 30 inches of snow on St. John's, the capital, and packed wind gusts as high as 81mph. The snowfall was an all-time record for the day for St. John's international airport. St. John's mayor, Danny Breen, said that a state of emergency remained in effect. Businesses were closed, as was the airport.

January 19

"Fore!" was the cry in Melbourne, Australia — not an alert from caddies but a reaction to "golf ball-sized hailstones" falling out of the sky, reported by The Guardian. Hail and torrential rain hit areas of New South Wales and southern Australia, notably damaging the roof of a local supermarket.

January 22

G L O R I A … Not a very popular name in eastern Spain this day as a so-named storm battered the country, resulting in nine people dead and four missing, according to The Guardian. High winds gusting up to 90mph, heavy rain, snowfall and huge waves (up to 44 feet high) also left 220,000 people in the Tarragona region without electricity.

Among the dead was a man who died of hypothermia in Carcaixent, Valencia; a woman killed in Alicante province when her home collapsed; a farmer in Almería who became trapped in a greenhouse during a hailstorm; and a man found in a flooded area a few miles inland from Benidorm.

January 23

Back here in Fairfield, CT, Fairfield HamletHub gave a "heads up" about a storm moving up from the Gulf of Mexico that was expected to impact the region with rain primarily.

January 24

Bug haters were horrified to learn of the billions of locusts swarming Kenya, reported by The Guardian. TG explained that the locusts in east Africa were the result of extreme weather swings and could prove catastrophic for a region still reeling from drought and deadly floods. Dense clouds of the ravenous insects had spread from Ethiopia and Somalia into Kenya, in the region's worse infestation in decades, noted TG.

January 25

Eastern Turkey got absolutely rocked by a 6.7-magnitude earthquake, that killed 22 people and injured more than 1,200, reported CNN. The quake struck near the town of Sivrice, in the country's Elazig province, collapsing at least 10 buildings, according to the Turkish Interior Minister. Eighteen people were killed in Elazig province and four in Malatya. Thirty-nine people were pulled from under the rubble of a collapsed building, the Minister said, adding that 22 other people remained trapped. The building was one of five to collapse in Elazig, while many other buildings sustained heavy damage. The initial quake lasted just 40 seconds. Fifteen aftershocks were felt in its wake, with the strongest registering at 5.4 magnitude.

January 28

Turkey was not the only area shaking this particular week. BBC News announced that a powerful 7.7-magnitude earthquake had struck in the Caribbean, prompting tsunami warnings and office evacuations as far away as Florida. The quake apparently hit between Jamaica, the Cayman Islands and Cuba at a depth of 6.2 miles, according to the US Geological Survey

(USGS). Buildings shook and tremors were felt across the Caribbean, but there were no immediate reports of casualties. Some offices were temporarily evacuated in Miami and parts of Jamaica. Warnings by the Pacific Tsunami Warning Center (PTWC) were later withdrawn. The USGS said this was the largest earthquake in the Caribbean since 1946.

January 29

Brazil got severely waterlogged, The Guardian said. Extreme rainfall (the city of Belo Horizonte received nearly seven inches, which was its largest daily rainfall total in 110 years of weather records) resulted in flooding and landslides in the southeastern part of the country, 30 people killed, 17 lost, and 2,600 evacuated from their homes.

January 31

Ana was bananas. Tropical Cyclone Ana, that is, which struck Fiji, according to The Guardian. One person died and five others, including a three-year-old boy, went missing. More than 10,000 people sought shelter in emergency evacuation centers. Torrential rain and strong winds caused severe flooding and widespread damage to buildings, crops and public infrastructure. Most of the country had both electricity and water service disruptions. TG said police in fiberglass boats were seen patrolling town centers as heavy downpours (coupled with high tides) overwhelmed drainage systems. Officers rescued two babies after a tree fell on the house where they had been sheltered.

Ana's visit came just over a month after Category 5 Cyclone Yasa tore through the country's northern islands. TG said that two additional cyclones were already forming off Fiji's coastline, with three months left yet of the traditional cyclone season.

February 6

January was hot, hot, hot in the U.S., reported the NOAA (National Oceanic and Atmospheric Administration). It was America's 5th warmest

January on record, in fact. All 48 contiguous states saw above- to much-above-average temperatures. January was also quite damp for the Lower 48, ranking it in the wettest third of all Januarys recorded in the 126-year climate record.

To get specific, the average January temperature across the contiguous U.S. was 35.5F (5.4 degrees above the 20th-century average). Much-above-average temperatures were observed across much of the Great Lakes and Northeast as well as parts of the Mid-Atlantic, Southeast, West and southern Plains.

January's precipitation for the contiguous U.S. was 2.70 inches (0.39 of an inch above average). January precipitation extended a noticeably wet 12-month stretch: February 2019 through January 2020 was the third-wettest such period ever recorded, 4.99 inches above average, according to the NOAA. Last month, much-above-average wetness was observed across the Pacific Northwest as well as portions of the central and southern U.S. Washington state experienced its fourth-wettest January, while Oklahoma saw its sixth wettest on record.

Some other notable NOAA observations:

- **A January that forgot it was winter**: No state in the Lower 48 ranked average or below average temperature-wise for January 2020. The month ranked as the fifth warmest January on record for Michigan, and the sixth warmest for Wisconsin and Rhode Island.
- **Great Lakes saw relatively low ice coverage**: Ice coverage was approximately 35 percent of average for January. Lake Erie, normally about 50 percent ice-covered by January 31, was only 0.4% frozen this year.
- **Alaska chilled out**: In stark contrast to the record warmth experienced during 2019, Alaska's average January temperature was a very frigid -6.2 degrees F — 8.4 degrees colder than the long-term mean. It was Alaska's coldest January since 2012.

February 7

More crazy weather in the southeast U.S., The Guardian said, reporting "at least five killed and 300,000 without power" resulting from a powerful storm that raked the region. Forecasters warned that the storm system could bring gusts of 50 to 60mph from the Carolinas into New England, potentially toppling rain-soaked trees and making driving hazardous.

At the same time, four inches of snow had fallen overnight in Ohio, part of a band of snowy weather stretching from Tennessee to Maine. Blowing snow contributed to several accidents in the Akron area. The Ohio department of transportation urged people to make room for nearly 1,300 state crews working to improve the icy conditions, TG detailed.

Later in the day in southwestern Connecticut, Fairfield HamletHub posted to Facebook, "Really blowing here in the Fairfield, CT area, with very strong wind gusts this afternoon. Be careful of falling limbs and downed wires! Have a plan if the power goes out." Snow joined the mix and temps quickly plummeted, adding to the hazards.

February 10

A viral challenge overtook Twitter feeds, featuring people balancing brooms upright in order to demonstrate a supposed unique gravitational pull taking place. It was initiated by Twitter user @mikaiylaaaaa, who shared, "Okay so NASA said today was the only day a broom can stand up on its own because of the gravitational pull." Her tweet accompanied a video of herself balancing a broom, along with the hashtag #BroomChallenge. Thousands of people uploaded their own videos of broom balancing acts. According to NASA though, the stunt's premise was false, related Science Alert.

"This is another social media hoax that exemplifies how quickly pseudoscience and false claims can go viral," NASA stated. "While this hoax was harmless, it also shows why it's important for all of us to do some fact-checking and research — including checking in with @NASA and NASA.gov for real science fun facts — before jumping into the latest viral craze."

Science Alert said NASA took the opportunity to educate on the platform that inspired the viral challenge in the first place. The NASA Twitter account posted a video of astronaut Drew Alvin and scientist Sarah Noble demonstrating the challenge, *the following day,* to show that "basic physics works every day of the year - not just February 10th."

February 17

It was the U.K.'s turn to get whacked, detailed by The Guardian. Storm Dennis — AKA Dennis the Menace — struck Wales, delivering heavy rain, wind and flooding, in particular to the town of Hay-on-Wye, on the Welsh side of the Welsh/English border. Footage posted on social media showed vehicles half-submerged and floating away after a nearby river burst its banks.

February 18

Welsh woes didn't stop with Dennis. A follow-up report by The Guardian warned that "parts of Wales that have been hit by the worst floods in a generation are preparing for further rain in the next 48 hours, as more than 450 flood warnings and alerts remain in place across the UK. Heavy rain is forecast in parts of north and south Wales, hampering the round-the-clock cleanup operation launched after Storm Dennis."

The Welsh Labour MP for Pontypridd, Alex Davies-Jones, told TG that stricken communities were refilling sandbags and repairing flood gates in anticipation of the next menace, Storm Ellen. "Homes have been completely destroyed, even those with flood gates," she said, adding that 600 people had been forced to evacuate their homes and more than 1,000 properties were badly damaged. "It's absolutely tragic. Heartbreaking."

In the meantime, Sydney, Australia, was having a bad time of things. Notably, a man was killed by a flying glass bottle as "NSW storms" moved through, The Guardian shared. The storms knocked out power to thousands of people and disrupted transport services, just weeks after record downpours caused major flooding. Damaging winds of about 68mph were reported at North Head, with other areas blasted by gusts over 62mph.

February 24

The Canaries were singing a sad song. The Canary Islands, that is, where The Guardian reported that a sandstorm had stranded tourists, forced the closure of airports, and cancelled scores of flights. Apparently, strong winds of up to 75mph had carried red sand from Africa's Sahara Desert across the water to the tourist hotspot. According to a CBS News affiliate, "Every now and then winds sweep across the Sahara desert to the northwest and vast amounts of sand and dust are carried offshore to the Canary Islands. Locals, however, say the current event is the worst in about 30 years."

February 26

It was hard not to cry for Argentina as heavy downpours caused flooding in South America, according to The Guardian. "Hundreds of people were evacuated from the northern provinces of Argentina" while "intense thunderstorms accompanied by hail and at least one tornado hit the province of Cordoba." Brazil and Paraguay were also affected, with landslides and flash-flooding causing widespread destruction.

February 27

The third storm in a month was stepping up to the wicket in the U.K., reported The Guardian. "Storm Jorge is expected to batter coastal areas with winds of up to 70mph, while downpours of over three inches could fall on already flooded areas," TG warned. Weather warnings were issued for parts of Wales and northern England, areas likely to see the worst of the rain and more flooding. The alerts followed a police warning to people living along the River Severn that they could face another 10 days of flooding misery, after water overwhelmed the flood barriers at Ironbridge, in Shropshire, forcing an emergency evacuation.

March 1

While the UK was getting more rain than it could handle, San Francisco went completely rain*less* in February, according to Weather. com. It was just the second time in the city's long weather history that it had a dry February. The only other completely dry February was in 1864, just 14 years after California became a state.

"February is in the heart of the Bay Area's wintertime wet season, so going rainless in the month is highly unusual," said Weather. "On average, San Francisco has nearly a dozen days with measurable rain in February. Including February 2020, the winter months of December, January and February have been rain-free a combined total of five times. A diversion of the jet stream is what made February so dry this year. High pressure aloft near or off the California coast was unusually strong, pushing the storm track northward into the Pacific Northwest."

March 4

Now *that's* a rock. Travel + Leisure shared that NASA was eyeing an asteroid half the height of Mt. Everest headed in the general direction of our Earth. Named 52768 (1998 OR2), the giant rock was not expected to make contact with our planet, but was big enough that a collision would cause "global effects." NASA estimated it was anywhere from 1.1 to 2.5 miles wide and projected it to pass within about 3.9 million miles of Earth on April 29, moving at a speed of about 19,460 miles per hour. The flyby was expected to happen at 4:56 a.m. ET.

T+L explained that the asteroid is tracked on NASA's list of potentially hazardous objects not because of its potential to collide with our planet but because of its size and the fact that it periodically passes by Earth.

March 10

"Lake Erie's Ice Machine Breaks", shared Weather.com. The headline was driven by the NOAA Great Lakes Environmental Research Laboratory's observation that Lake Erie was ice free from Dec. 29 through Jan. 17 and then again for four days after Groundhog Day. After spiking briefly to just under 16% ice coverage on Leap Day, the lake was ice free for the season beginning today. Typically, the lake reaches a peak of 70% ice coverage in February and isn't ice free until late April.

March 17

On St. Patrick's Day morning, a pair of tornado warnings were issued by the National Weather Service in the western Hawaiian Islands, said Weather.com. Since 1986, only two tornado warnings had previously been issued in Hawaii, the most recent one in December 2008.

While no tornadoes were confirmed, Doppler radar showed strong rotation. The last confirmed tornado in Hawaii was an EF0 land spout on Oahu on April 23, 2015.

March 18

Utah was holy rolling as a 5.7-magnitude earthquake hit, knocking out power to tens of thousands of people and diverting flights, according to CNN. Centered in the Salt Lake City area, the quake also suspended work at Utah's public health lab amid the coronavirus pandemic, officials said. "It didn't feel like a small earthquake at all," said one local. "I heard things in my kitchen falling." This was the state's most powerful quake since 1992, when a magnitude 5.9 temblor struck the St. George area, Utah's Division of Emergency Management told CNN.

And as Utah was shaking, central Tennessee was getting whipped, by devastating tornadoes, The Guardian said. At least 25 people were killed and a trail of homes and businesses were destroyed. The storms were the strongest to hit the region in almost a decade, with recorded wind speeds as high as 165mph. Trees were knocked down and power supplies were also disrupted. John C. Tune airport in Nashville also suffered extensive damage, with almost 100 aircraft damaged or destroyed, TG shared.

March 20

A funny thing happens when people aren't out and about much, like during pandemic-forced lockdowns the world over. "In countries like Japan, Italy, and Thailand, people observed animals roaming the streets due to human absence," said Bored Panda. "Like in Japan, where deer that are local to Nara Park were observed taking to the streets in search of food. Usually, the park is swarming with tourists, as the Sika deer living there are a local attraction. Tourists would usually buy crackers sold at the park meant specifically to feed the deer. However, as the number of visitors plummeted in recent weeks, the deer seem to have no choice but to wander out of their territory to find something to munch on."

Volcanoes, Hurricanes & Murder Hornets

April 1

Cities around the world weren't the only still places during our pandemic lockdown. The whole Earth *itself* had literally become more still, shared Popular Mechanics. In general, "Human activity of all kinds, as we travel and gather and drive around, generates vibrations that distort measurements from finely tuned seismic instruments," PM said. Scientists found that our protective self-quarantine had reduced that ambient seismic noise. In Belgium, for instance, scientists reported a 30 percent reduction since the Covid-19 lockdown began there. The resulting quiet meant surface seismic readings had become as clear as the ones scientists would usually get from the same instruments buried 325 feet beneath the Earth's surface, which make measurements more specific and easier to use and understand. To interpret the change another way: a much quieter Earth was giving measurements similar to ones a hypothetical 19th century scientist might observe. Further, it was suggested that having that data as a comparison point could prove useful going forward.

April 2

Moonie, Moonie, Moonie. Travel + Leisure promised "The Biggest Full Moon of the Year" to rise April 7. There had already been two supermoons since 2020's start — a "Super Snow Moon" in February and "Super Worm Moon" in March — but those were "mere celestial warm-up acts" apparently. T+L promised April's "Super Pink Moon" would be the biggest, brightest and best supermoon of the year, given that it would be closer to us than any other time during the year and so appear to be around 14% bigger in apparent size. And why the "Pink" assignation? Its appearance coincided with the springtime blooms of the "moss pink" wildflower.

April 5

So, parts of the world had deer rambling in their quiet cities. But did they have mobs of *nut gatherers*? TMZ reported "Santa Monica parks are no longer filled with humans. They're being overrun by a gaggle of squirrels." The normally celeb-focused news purveyor even shared a video to its online site of "the furry little critters chilling out and catching some rays in the parks along the world-famous Santa Monica Beach." Further, TMZ made a comparison that "the squirrel scene is reminiscent of what we've already seen over in Wales, where an entire town is being overrun by goats as humans shelter in place."

April 10

A very worrying fatal and infectious bird flu was confirmed in a commercial turkey flock in South Carolina, reported PBS NEWS HOUR. It was the first case of the serious strain detected in the United States since one found in a Tennessee chicken flock in 2017. The latest high pathogenic case was discovered at an operation in Chesterfield County, SC, and confirmed by a lab in Ames, Iowa to be a H7N3 strain of avian influenza. The strain killed 1,583 turkeys in the flock; the remainder of the 32,577 birds at the operation were euthanized. State officials quarantined the farm, implemented movement controls, and put enhanced surveillance in place in the area. For reference, in 2015, an estimated 50 million poultry had to be killed at operations mainly in America's Upper Midwest after infections spread throughout the region.

On the B side of the world, Krakatoa volcano, in Indonesia, blew its stack, said the Daily Mail. The volcano spewed plumes of ash 1,600 feet into the air and was heard rumbling as far as 90 miles away in Jakarta. Satellite imagery captured plumes and lava flows coming from the crater. It was the site's first eruption since December 2018, which caused a tsunami killing over 400 people. The volcano's historic 1883 eruption killed more than 36,000 people.

April 12

Easter wasn't all egg hunts and hams for peeps in America's South, as tornadoes and severe weather struck multiple states, said FOX News. National Weather Service (NWS) officials confirmed 13 tornadoes had appeared in Mississippi and Louisiana, and that two tornadoes hit Texas. The city of Monroe, La., shared on Twitter "reports of damage in multiple neighborhoods" after the storm moved through. The NWS said 20 homes in one subdivision were reported to have sustained damage and multiple planes and hangars suffered damage at the Monroe Regional Airport. A photo from the city showed damage at the airport, including several aircraft that appeared to be overturned. Other images from the city revealed downed power lines in various areas.

April 13

Southwestern Connecticut got a taste of Southern weather when a powerful storm pushed through the region, reported Fairfield, CT's Fairfield HamletHub. Local electricity provider United Illuminating said over 700 of its customers had lost power as of midday. Across all of Connecticut, over 17,000 people lost power, which compounded the hardship of being homebound due to the coronavirus.

Meanwhile, tornadoes continued to impact the South. WSB-TV Atlanta reported eight people had been killed in northern Georgia. Seven of those victims were killed in Murray County when several mobile homes were flattened. The other victim was killed in Bartow County when a tree fell on his home. The National Weather Service confirmed the killer as an EF-1 tornado, with winds up to 90 mph. Tornadoes were also reported in Thomaston, South Fulton, Putnam and Chattooga counties.

April 14

Talk about getting an alignment... India Times offered a heads-up about a "rare event": Jupiter, Saturn, Mars and the moon appearing together for three days, April 14, 15, and 16. The news service explained, "Jupiter, Saturn and Mars are morning planets, which means they are easier to spot in the morning. The three planets have been stretching out gradually and, in the middle of April, the three would almost be in a single line, highlighted by the moon."

IT suggested the sight would be particularly easy to see at this moment in time: "One of the side effects of the coronavirus lockdown around the world has been the tremendous reduction in pollution level. One can breathe in fresh air. And after ages probably, stars are also visible in the night sky. This is an ideal time to stargaze."

April 16

The San Francisco Chronicle related that California — and the rest of the West — could be on a "troubling long-term skid into drier times." According to a group of scientists, the region has been in the midst of a prolonged drought since the beginning of the century — one on par with only four mega-droughts experienced over the past 1,200 years and one capable of causing major social upheaval. The last mega-drought that the researchers describe, between 1575 and 1593, is believed to have forced Native Americans to relocate whole communities from sprawling mesas to lower river valleys in search of water. The mega-drought before that, in the 1200s, is thought to have contributed to the fall of the cliff-dwelling Anasazi civilization in the Southwest.

"The past two decades look a lot like how the biggest mega-droughts of the past millennium developed," said Park Williams, bio-climatologist at Columbia University's Lamont-Doherty Earth Observatory and lead author of the study. "These mega-droughts are not like anything we've seen in recent centuries. They're viewed as mythical beasts. There's nothing that's come even close to them."

The fear, according to the article, was that, if current dry times continued, which the paper's authors thought was more likely than not, the modern era soon would soon be in the grip of its first mega-drought.

On a separate but uplifting note, NBC Los Angeles shared that, "for the first time in decades, bald eagles have been found nesting in an Arizona saguaro cactus." The Arizona Game and Fish Department revealed that biologists discovered a pair of eagles and their eaglets in the arms of a large saguaro during a recent eagle survey. Photos the agency posted showed the eagles nestled at the base of the cactus arm. Wildlife biologists had apparently been looking for decades for this scenario, not seen since 1937.

And in the heavens beyond, C/NET shared that NASA had discovered an exoplanet remarkably like ours, giving hope for a "second Earth". The planet's existence was discovered in old data generated by NASA's now retired Kepler Space Telescope, which went on an epic hunt for planets beyond our own solar system before it "ran out of fuel and went to sleep in 2018."

The exoplanet, Kepler-1649c, is located 300 light-years from Earth. NASA described it as the "most similar to Earth in size and estimated temperature" out of the thousands of exoplanets discovered by Kepler. The planet is located in its star's habitable zone, a region where it's possible for liquid water to exist.

C/NET related that "the fascinating exoplanet is slightly larger than Earth. It receives 75% of the amount of light we get from our own sun, which could put it in line with Earth temperatures as well. The planet was originally misidentified by a computer algorithm, but a team of scientists found it during a review of Kepler data." The downside: Kepler-1649c is in orbit around a red dwarf, a type of star that NASA said "is known for stellar flare-ups that may make a planet's environment challenging for any potential life." The space agency also cautioned that Kepler-1649c's atmosphere is still a mystery and that the size calculations may be off.

April 20

The Weather Channel warned that, while the 2020 Atlantic hurricane season was one month away, the past five seasons have each gotten off to an early start. Officially, the Atlantic hurricane season runs from June 1 through Nov. 30. That timeframe was selected to encompass 97% of all

Atlantic tropical storms and hurricanes, according to NOAA's Hurricane Research Division. However, a small number of tropical storms, even hurricanes, have occurred primarily in May and December, but also in every other month outside of hurricane season. Since 2015, at least one named storm has developed before June 1 each hurricane season, some of which had impacts in the United States and elsewhere in the Atlantic Basin.

In May 2019, Subtropical Storm Andrea formed southwest of Bermuda the week before Memorial Day, but only lasted about 24 hours. In 2018, Tropical Storm Alberto made a Memorial Day landfall along the Florida Panhandle, remained intact, and took a strange track into Lower Michigan before losing its tropical characteristics. Tropical Storm Arlene developed even earlier than Alberto and, in 2017, became only the second April Atlantic tropical storm of record. Perhaps 2016 was the strangest early start to an Atlantic season in recent memory, though, TWC suggested. Tropical Storm Bonnie soaked the coast of the Carolinas in late May that year. But that was preceded by eastern Atlantic Hurricane Alex, only the second known January Atlantic hurricane. Alex eventually made landfall in the Azores as a tropical storm.

TWC shared more historical record breakers. In 2015, Tropical Storm Ana made the second-earliest U.S. landfall of at least a tropical storm on Mother's Day weekend along the coast of the Carolinas. This early start also happened in 2012 (Alberto, then Beryl in May), 2008 (Arthur), 2007 (another Subtropical Storm Andrea) and 2003 (another Ana, this time in April). Beryl nearly became a hurricane before coming ashore near Jacksonville Beach, Florida, on Memorial Day weekend 2012.

Nine of 17 years from 2003 through 2019, though, had at least one named storm before June 1, and there were a total of 11 out-of-season named storms during that time. The majority of these developed and meandered, or made landfall along the coast from North Carolina to northeastern Florida.

April 21

Space.com told us to look up as the Lyrid meteor shower of 2020 was peaking. The star-gazing group promised, "Without any glaring moonlight to obstruct the view, skywatchers will have an excellent view this year — weather permitting." In a dark, clear sky, observers in the Northern Hemisphere were expected to see as many as 10 to 20 meteors per hour during the shower's peak.

April 23

A string of tornadoes pummeled the South, said ABC News. "At least 26 tornadoes have been reported now in Oklahoma, Texas, Louisiana and Mississippi with at least six people killed by the severe weather since yesterday," ABC detailed. "Some of the worst damage from tornadoes was from southern Oklahoma into eastern Texas and through central Louisiana."

A watch was issued for additional tornadoes in Louisiana, Mississippi, Alabama and Florida, as well as for the stretch from Atlanta to Tallahassee, and Jacksonville, Florida, into Charleston, South Carolina. In addition to tornadoes, damaging straight-line winds near 70 mph were expected, with golf ball-sized hail and flash flooding.

April 25

Chalk this one up in the weather history books: "Eastern Pacific Tropical Depression a First For April", headlined Weather.com. "While not quite as rare in the Atlantic Basin, no tropical depression, storm or hurricane had been documented in April over the eastern Pacific Ocean since the mid-20th century," Weather stated. Until 2020, that is, and Tropical Depression One-E, which popped up south of Mexico's Baja California Peninsula. Though it only lasted 18 hours, it was still the basin's first April tropical cyclone of record. Before One-E, the earliest Eastern Pacific tropical depression or storm was Tropical Storm Adrian, which formed off the coast of El Salvador and Guatemala on May 9, 2017.

April 27

The Guardian gave an early heads-up that 2020 was on course to be the hottest year since records began. The prediction was ventured by meteorologists, who estimated there was a 50-75% chance that 2020 would break the record set four years ago.

"Although the coronavirus lockdown has temporarily cleared the skies, it has done nothing to cool the climate, which needs deeper, longer-term measures," said scientists, according to TG. Heat records had already been broken from the Antarctic to Greenland since January, which surprised many scientists because this was not an El Niño year, the phenomenon usually associated with high temperatures. The US National Oceanic and Atmospheric Administration said trends were closely tracking 2016's record, when temperatures soared early in the year due to an unusually intense El Niño and then came down.

Somalia, in the meantime, was in a bad way, pummeled by deadly flash floods, said FloodList. "Heavy rain has affected wide areas of Somalia since April 20, causing rivers to rise and flash flooding. According to reports from the United Nations, tens of thousands of people have been affected or displaced."

Notably, massive flash flooding swept through the city of Qardho in the northeastern Bari region, part of the autonomous Puntland state. At least six people died, several others went missing and hundreds of families had reportedly lost their homes. Heavy rain also caused flooding in Baidoa, South West State, Bay Region, destroying the shelters of more than 81,000 individuals (13,582 households) living in 73 settlements for internally displaced people (IDPs).

In Jubaland, some 300 households were affected by the river flooding in Bardheere district. Some farmers in Bardheere town lost most of their crops. In Dhobley, Afmadow, ongoing rains affected about 2,000 displaced households in Danwadaag IDP settlement. The impacted households moved to nearby areas but did not have access to shelter.

In other news of the day, the U.S. Department of Defense *officially* allowed the release of three unclassified Navy videos, one taken in November 2004 and the other two in January 2015, showing "unidentified" flying objects. The videos had already been circulating in the public domain — the

DOD basically confirmed their authenticity as unexplained phenomena. So there was *that* to twist our imaginations.

May 1

Cicada swarms? Really? Our Community Now alerted that, with Spring's arrival, 17-year cicadas were going to emerge and occupy Virginia, West Virginia and North Carolina. These "periodical" cicadas — a different breed than the traditional green cicadas that Americans see every year — were expected to number in the hundreds of millions.

There was a swarm of a watery kind further south: "Five Tornadoes at Once", Weather.com related. A Televisa correspondent captured video of multiple landspout tornadoes in Mexico's Puebla state, between Mexico City and Veracruz. These landspouts occur when a growing thunderstorm's rising air vertically stretches spin along a boundary of convergent winds. In this case, there were multiple thunderstorms growing along such a boundary, leading to this incredible sight of five landspouts.

Meanwhile, other "useful" swarms were dying, said The Guardian, reporting that a viral disease that causes honey bees to suffer severe trembling, flightlessness and death within a week was spreading exponentially in Britain. "Chronic bee paralysis virus (CBPV) was first recorded in Lincolnshire in 2007. A decade later, it was found in 39 of 47 English counties and six of eight Welsh counties, according to data collected from visits to more than 24,000 beekeepers. As well as struggling to fly, the afflicted bees develop shiny, hairless abdomens. Piles of dead individuals are found outside hives with whole colonies frequently wiped out by the disease," TG shared. Scientists studying the disease found it was nearly twice as likely in apiaries owned by beekeepers who import honey bees to replenish their hives every few years.

May 2

Another story getting a lot of buzz? Asian Murder Hornets were found in the U.S. for the first time, the New York Post shared. "Enough already," the story led. "Now, deadly hornets from Asia that measure up to two inches long have been found for the first time in the U.S. — and researchers are worried they're colonizing. The aggressive insects can wipe out bee colonies within hours and have stingers long and powerful enough to puncture beekeeping suits. Beekeepers in Washington have already seen the hornets devastate their hives; Japan attributes 50 human deaths a year to the nasty buzzers, which have 'teardrop eyes like Spider-Man, orange and black stripes that extend down its body like a tiger, and broad, wispy wings like a small dragonfly.'" Researchers said they were determined to keep the hornets in check.

May 4

Police in Walker, Alabama, were searching for an "aggressive chicken" that had been attacking people at ATMs, according to MyStateline. com. Witnesses told police the fowl had been spotted at a local bank multiple times in the past week, approaching patrons at the ATM, chasing customers, and even attempting to climb into cars in the drive-thru. Police advised residents to avoid confronting the animal.

May 5

Environmental org Save the Sound announced that, between May 6 and 8, shorelines on both sides of Long Island Sound (the north shore of Long Island, NY, and the southwestern shore of Connecticut) would be experiencing King Tides — the highest regional tides of the year due to the alignment of both the sun and the moon's gravitational pull. The group asked shoreline residents to take photos of the shore during that time, to better document its effects. The group explained that the feedback would be vital for regional planners to assess the extent of local flooding and the potential effects of sea level rise.

May 6

The Washington Post alerted readers that the Polar Vortex was about to unleash winter-like cold across half the U.S. "After remaining well-behaved all winter, the mischievous Polar Vortex is set to thrust a lobe of frigid, wintry air south over the eastern United States, bringing snow to places in the Northeast and Mid-Atlantic, and chilly temperatures from the Upper Midwest to New England. Frost could even visit places such as northern Georgia and the western Carolinas as the expansive cold air mass settles south and challenges records. Temperatures in many places will feel more like early March than early May," WP said.

The paper detailed, "A dollop of wintry mischief, including the potential for a few areas of accumulating snow, is on tap along the Appalachians from North Carolina through Maine. In some areas, a coating or more of snow is possible — especially across central and northern New England. Even where the flakes don't fly, temperatures will still sit some 20 degrees or more below average as a strong cold front slides all the way down near the Gulf Coast, with temperatures falling into the 30s and 40s in its wake. Mother's Day could feel more like St. Patrick's Day in some areas before a gradual recovery occurs next week."

That announcement didn't seem to have any bearing further south, in northwest Florida, where USA Today said the Five-Mile Swamp Fire was raging out of control, forcing 1,100 evacuations from Santa Rosa County and a partial closure of Interstate 10. Fueled by high winds and low humidity, the fire, which began as a prescribed burn on private property, was stoked by drought conditions and a northerly wind.

"This is a significant fire event," said a spokesman for the Florida Forest Service. "Deteriorating weather conditions, changes in the wind, a strong north wind and extremely low humidity are allowing this fire to grow." Florida's chief financial officer and state fire marshal, Jimmy Patronis, tweeted that the fire had grown to more than 2,000 acres.

May 8

As if Washington state didn't have enough to worry about with Murder Hornets, now it had non-native Gypsy moths to contend with, said CNN. The discovery was such a threat, in fact, that Gov. Jay Inslee issued an emergency proclamation, saying there was an "imminent danger of an infestation" in parts of Snohomish County. Inslee said the threat "seriously endangers the agricultural and horticultural industries of the state of

Washington and seriously threatens the economic well-being and quality of life of state residents." The plant predators included both Asian gypsy moths and Asian-European hybrid gypsy moths.

According to the U.S. Dept. of Agriculture's Animal and Plant Health Inspection Service, "Large (Asian gypsy moth) infestations can completely defoliate trees", severely weaken them (as well as shrubs), and make them more susceptible to disease. Repeated defoliation can lead to the death of large sections of forests, orchards and landscaping.

CNN detailed that females can lay hundreds of eggs, which become caterpillars and munch through more than 500 different tree and shrub species. And because the moths can fly long distances, it was likely they could quickly spread throughout the country.

May 9

Snow fell in Central Park, tying a 1977 record for the latest snow in a season in that area, according to 1010 WINS. The National Weather Service said a "trace" of snow was recorded, meaning there was precipitation but it was not measurable.

The same weather pattern that delivered the Central Park flakes also delivered teeth-rattling cold to the East, Midwest and South for Mother's Day weekend, said Weather.com. Van Wert, Ohio, for instance, plunged to 18 degrees, the first time it had dropped into the teens in May in 127 years of records. All-time May records were also set in Binghamton, New York; Fort Wayne, Indiana; Indianapolis; and New York's LaGuardia Airport.

Weather.com added that Detroit picked up at least a trace of snow five straight days, a May record, and that the cold pattern also prompted the first May winter storm warning issued by the NWS in Caribou, Maine, in at least 15 years.

May 10

Extremes were not exclusive to the north. CNN reported record temperatures and dry weather in Florida. "Florida is known for its hot weather, but this year has been exceptionally torrid. In April, South Florida hit June-like temperatures. Miami, in fact, had seen 16 days with high temperatures at or above 90 degrees from January 1 through the end of April. The city normally only averages two 90-degree days during that period," said CNN. In April, Miami didn't have a single day where temperatures fell below average. In fact, more than half of the month saw temperatures at least five degrees above average. More impressive was that Miami had 14 days of record highs in April. On April 20, the temperature hit 97 degrees, breaking the city's previous all-time high of 96 degrees, which was set in 2015.

Florida was also lacking rain. Orlando and West Palm Beach were seven inches below normal for rainfall for the year. Daytona and Fort Myers had deficits around six inches.

Out on the West coast, tragically, a 26-year-old surfer was killed in a California shark attack, said CNN. The man was mauled at Manresa State Beach, the California Department of Parks and Recreation stated, within 100 yards of the shore, and pronounced dead on the scene.

And across the world, Typhoon Ambo made landfall in the Philippines, reported AccuWeather. Its landing was the first of numerous expected landfalls over the eastern Philippines as the storm forged a path of destruction over the northern islands. Ambo was packing sustained winds of 96mph, a strength equivalent to a Category 3 hurricane in the Atlantic and East Pacific basins.

May 12

A gigantic new swarm of locusts was ravaging East Africa, said National Geographic. "These...swarms...are terrifying," a local man said as he recorded a video of himself swatting his way through a crush of desert locusts in northern Kenya in April. More than two inches long, the insects whirred around him in thick clouds, their wings snapping like ten thousand card decks being shuffled in unison, as CNN described it. He groaned: "They are in the millions. Everywhere...eating...it really is a nightmare."

With their seemingly bottomless appetites, locusts can cause devastating agricultural losses. CNN offered stats: An adult desert locust can munch through its own bodyweight, about 0.07 ounces, of vegetation every day. Swarms can swell to 70 billion insects — enough to blanket New York City more than once — and can destroy 300 million pounds of crops in a single day. Even a more modest gathering of 40 million desert locusts can eat as much in a day as 35,000 people.

The "upsurge"— on an intensity just below "plague" level — was the worst experienced in Ethiopia and Somalia for 25 years and in Kenya for 70 years. The region's growing season had just gotten underway. With the swarms growing and the coronavirus complicating mitigation efforts, the United Nations Food and Agriculture Organization (FAO) estimated up to 25 million East Africans would suffer from food shortages later this year.

Already, some 13 million people in Ethiopia, Kenya, Somalia, Djibouti, and Eritrea were suffering from "severe food insecurity," according to the FAO, going without eating for an entire day or without food altogether.

May 15

An earthquake with a magnitude of 6.5 hit Nevada, reported AccuWeather. The epicenter was located about 225 miles northwest of Las Vegas near the California border, the US Geological Survey said. At least four aftershocks were reported. Officials were assessing structures for damage.

May 16

High winds and heavy rain caused widespread damage and 35,000 customers to lose their electricity across New England, the Daily Mail shared.

In Holyoke, Massachusetts, the roof was ripped off an apartment building, sending debris flying onto cars parked below. The damage left 141 residents of the building homeless overnight. Across that state, 28,000 lost power.

New Hampshire authorities reported around 3,000 residents without power; 3,800 customers in Vermont lost power, too.

In some parts of the region, wind gusts reached 56mph. There were also several reports of downed trees and wires in residential areas.

Tornado warnings were activated for southern Vermont and New Hampshire. Residents of Vermont, Massachusetts, New Hampshire, Connecticut, and Rhode Island all received severe thunderstorm alerts on their cell phones, as well.

Severe weather was also observed in the Hudson Valley region of New York State, parts of which were under a tornado watch.

Meteorologists said the severe weather was due to a low pressure system that formed as a result of unseasonably warm temperatures.

Meanwhile, the air over the Gulf of Mexico region had become particularly moist, said the Daily Mail, creating conditions for even more severe weather after a week of heavy rains resulted in flash flooding in parts of the southern Plains including Texas, Kansas and Louisiana. Cars had become stranded in several inches of water near Houston as flash floods inundated parts of the Lone Star State. In neighboring Oklahoma, at least 5,000 people were left without power as severe storms led to flash flooding.

May 20

In southwestern Connecticut, Fairfield HamletHub told followers to look out for a sunset planet show. "About 30 minutes after sunset, look toward the low western sky for an impressive close encounter between our solar system's two innermost planets, Venus and Mercury. They will appear closest together about 45 minutes to an hour after sunset on May 21, when they will be separated by about one arc-degree — equal to the width of your little finger or index finger held at arm's length."

Meanwhile, Michigan Governor Gretchen Whitmer had declared an emergency in her state and warned Midland County area residents "do not hesitate" to evacuate, forecasting that the area could soon find itself under nine feet of water, USA Today related. Her alert followed the breach of dams in Edenville and Sanford after four to seven inches of rain fell in one compressed stretch of time. In particular, tens of thousands of people were potentially in harm's way due to flooding along the Tittabawassee River.

"This is unlike anything we've seen before... but this is truly a historic event that's playing out in the midst of another historic event," Whitmer said, referring to the coronavirus pandemic which had led to stay-at-home orders throughout the state and the deaths of more than 5,000 people.

And while Michiganders were getting waterlogged, Southwest Asia was getting clobbered again, said The Guardian, by Super-Cyclone Amphan, which hit the coast of India and Bangladesh. The Bay of Bengal's fiercest storm this century, Amphan made landfall with winds of about 120mph, causing storm surges of up to 17 feet, before moving northwards towards Kolkata, one of India's biggest cities. Two deaths were reported in Bangladesh, where more than two million people had been evacuated. Three deaths occurred in West Bengal, where half a million people were moved from vulnerable low-lying areas to shelters. The Indian navy was made ready to offer humanitarian assistance. Amphan claimed the distinction of being only the second "super-cyclone" to form in the Bay of Bengal since records began.

Complicating matters was the pandemic. "It is another form of new normal, that we have to handle disasters considering the pandemic, too. In view of the prevailing Covid-19 scenario, all teams are equipped with PPE [personal protective equipment]," said the director general of the National Disaster Response Force (NDRF), SN Pradhan.

May 25

Green Eggs & Ham really did happen… the green eggs part, anyhow, said The Guardian. A chicken farmer from Malappuram, India, confirmed that some of his poultry were laying eggs with green egg yolks. Initially, when photos of the chicken eggs with dark green yolks surfaced online, many thought the images were digitally manipulated. However, when the photos were traced back to the farmer, he confirmed their authenticity by sharing a video of himself cracking open an egg and revealing the dark green yolk.

"We were astonished at first, and did not use the egg to consume," said the farmer. "All the eggs which the hen laid were this kind and so we started to incubate the eggs. Out of the six chicks which hatched from these eggs, a few have started to lay eggs and those yolks are also green in color."

The farmer also confirmed that neither he nor his family had shown strange symptoms since consuming the eggs, which he said tasted just like normal eggs.

Veterinary experts suggested there was a high possibility that the anomaly might be caused by the feed given to the birds, though the farmer claimed all the poultry were fed just organic matter: rice, coconut oil cake and organic kitchen waste from his house.

May 27

The very north of India, New Delhi, was suffering from a myriad of miseries: a heatwave, super hot winds, the coronavirus pandemic, wildfires in the Uttarakhand forest, and swarms of desert locusts. The heatwave alone defined the region for a 24-hour period as the hottest on the planet, and was accelerating the forest fires. Many acres of green cover had been gutted and resident animals were struggling hard to stay alive as water sources dried up or were fouled. A total of 46 fires had been reported in Uttarakhand; two-dozen more fires were burning in the Kumaon region.

May 29

Live Science reported some troubling monkey business: a primate had attacked a lab technician on the campus of a government-run medical school in Uttar Pradesh, India, and run away with blood samples from three patients infected with Covid-19. The lab tech captured a video of the incident with his phone revealing the monkey clambering up a nearby tree and gnawing on what appeared to be surgical gloves.

Local residents were concerned the event might increase the risk of virus transmission — first to other monkeys and then to humans. To this point, there were 7,170 confirmed cases of Covid-19 in the region. It was proven that humans could infect some animals with SARS-CoV-2, the novel coronavirus that caused the Covid-19 disease. In April, five tigers and three lions at the Bronx Zoo in New York City tested positive for the coronavirus; they were infected by an asymptomatic staff person, according to the Wildlife Conservation Society. Two pet cats and a pet dog in the U.S. had also tested positive for the coronavirus, which they likely contracted from contact with people. And SARS-CoV-2 vaccine candidates had been tested on rhesus macaques, which showed symptoms of the disease. However, the monkey snatched blood samples, and not throat or tongue swabs from infected patients, the medical college's principal assured.

Ticks, Sharks & Jellyfish

June 1

Tropical Storm Cristobal became the third named storm of the 2020 Atlantic hurricane season, and the earliest third named storm in the North Atlantic Ocean on record, eclipsing the date set by Tropical Storm Colin in 2016, which formed on June 5, confirmed Wikipedia. It was also the first Atlantic tropical cyclone to form in the month of June since Cindy in 2017, *and* the first June tropical cyclone to make landfall in Mexico since Danielle in 2016.

June 6

Giddyup! The southwestern United States had a derecho running wild through its canyon lands, said Weather.com. A new term to many when it was announced, a derecho is defined as a long line of severe thunderstorms producing damaging winds, most common in the Plains, Midwest and South. On the first Saturday in June, however, a derecho broke out of its corral in Utah, then raced 750 miles northeast into the Dakotas, in just 12 hours. NOAA's Storm Prediction Center noted it was only the third derecho ever documented west of the Rockies. The SPC also noted this derecho produced the most 75 mph or stronger thunderstorm wind gusts in a single day since at least 2004. A gust to 110 mph was measured near Winter Park, Colorado.

June 10

Tropical Storm Cristobal went on a Midwest adventure, said Weather. com, ambling up from the Gulf of Mexico, all the way to Wisconsin. Before Cristobal, the remnants of just three other Atlantic tropical cyclones had tracked through Wisconsin or its adjacent Lake Michigan waters in more than 100 years of records. The other three remnant systems were Gilbert in 1988, an unnamed former hurricane in 1949, and the Galveston Hurricane of 1900, the nation's deadliest. Cristobal was different from those systems, said Weather.com, because its remnants traversed the entire length of Wisconsin to the Upper Peninsula of the Michigan border. That was the farthest west on record a tropical cyclone remnant from the Atlantic Basin had tracked through the Badger State.

June 12

Connecticut had its own horseplay to contend with — quelling Eastern equine encephalitis (EEE) to prevent a potential late summer outbreak, indicated WTNH News 8 CT. The state was preparing for a possible spike in EEE come late summer. Scientists at the Agricultural Experiment Station in New Haven had been studying mosquitoes and trapping them daily in areas around the state, especially in eastern Connecticut where they're known to thrive. In 2019, scientists saw an exceptionally high number of mosquitoes carrying the rare, yet deadly virus. Unlike the novel coronavirus, scientists said EEE has lingering effects on all age groups; about a third of hospitalized cases die from the infection.

While CT was bugging out, New York had its hands full with ticks. FOX 32 Chicago reported that a tick-borne disease with symptoms similar to Covid-19 was on the rise in the state. Called anaplasmosis, the disease is caused by a bacteria spread to people through tick bites, according to the Centers for Disease Control and Prevention. Some of the symptoms can include fever, headache, chills and muscle aches — which are also similar signs of the coronavirus, as listed by the CDC.

"That's one that's really on the rise, particularly in the northeastern part of New York," Byron Backenson, deputy director of the state Health Department's Bureau of Communicable Disease Control, stated. The onset of symptoms usually begins one to two weeks after the bite of an infected tick. And, while rare, anaplasmosis can be fatal if left untreated.

Backenson noted the difficulty in informing the public about the increase of anaplasmosis amid the ongoing global pandemic. He said the condition was also often overshadowed by Lyme disease — the most prevalent tick-borne illness in New York, with more than 5,500 new cases each year. Not including New York City, the state saw about 300 human cases of anaplasmosis in 2009. By 2018, records show that cases had more than tripled. Unlike Lyme disease, the test for anaplasmosis was easy, and the disease could be muted with antibiotics.

Mosquitos to the left, ticks to the right, and tornadoes across the pond. The Washington Post alerted that rare tornadoes were possible in Britain over the coming weekend as severe storms struck.

Britain averages a little more than 30 tornadoes per year, shared WP. "Most are quick-hitting and weak, causing little damage. It's not often that conditions come together to support a forecast of tornado activity. But a couple of twisters — and associated rotating supercell thunderstorms — are possible in parts of Britain," the paper said. Southwestern England and southern Wales were pegged as the first area of risk, then northern Wales and northwestern England. Strong to severe thunderstorms with wind and hail were possible for Ireland and Northern Ireland as well.

June 16

In our Fairfield, CT area, the Fairfield Beach Residents Association echoed weather forecaster predictions that "an above-normal 2020 Atlantic hurricane season is expected, according to forecasters with NOAA's Climate Prediction Center, a division of the National Weather Service. The outlook predicts a 60% chance of an above-normal season, a 30% chance of a near-normal season and only a 10% chance of a below-normal season." Already we had seen the stirrings, eg. Cristobal, on June 10.

June 18

The cacti were cooking, literally, due in large part to the "Bush Fire" raging in Arizona, that had quickly doubled in size and forced evacuations, according to ABC News. The fire had become the largest in the country, encompassing 104,379 acres — and it was only 5% contained. New evacuations were issued for a second conflagration, the "Mangum Fire", in northern Arizona, which had grown to 56,780 acres and was only 3% contained. A third spark-up nearby, the "Big Horn Fire", had burned at least 23,892 acres and was 40% contained. Weather watchers expected regional windy conditions to subside as a huge ridge of high pressure moved into the area, which would help with containment.

June 19

Who could imagine that Northern Maine would claim the title for a day of being the Nation's Hot Spot? Weather.com related that, the week before Father's Day, Caribou, Maine, one of the farthest-north towns in the continental U.S., was one of the hottest places east of the Mississippi River. Temperatures soared to 95 degrees yesterday, then 96 degrees today. The city tied its all-time heat record dating back to 1939. It was the only area in the nation where there was a heat advisory for the day. Including this hot stretch, Caribou had as many 90-degree days through June 19 as Birmingham, Alabama. That was rather remarkable given that Caribou's *average* high in mid-June is in the low 70s.

As this phenomenon was happening way up north, parts of the typically hot Carolinas saw consecutive days of record-cool seasonal temperatures. Florence, North Carolina, for instance, stayed below 70 degrees for 43 straight hours. Only 1967 and 1997 saw longer June streaks there, according to Weather.com.

At the same time, Science Alert reported a "spectacular fireball" shooting across the sky over Western Australia. SA related the event through the perspective of a local: It was early morning when Denby Turton, a mechanical fitter at the Yandi mine in Western Australia, saw a curious light streaking through the sky. He and three others were sitting on top of a crusher, waiting for it to start up, when his boss suddenly exclaimed, "What the heck is that?" He turned, just in time to see and film a flaming ball of greenish blue shoot across the night. "It went for ages, super slow," recalled Turton. "We all couldn't believe our eyes."

Because of the remoteness of the sighting, there were no established science organization cameras monitoring the heavens. As such, astronomers weren't sure if the sight was a meteorite burning up in our atmosphere or something else, like a piece of blazing space junk.

June 20

Is it hot in here, or is that just Siberia, Weather.com wondered, sharing that, on this day, the high temperature in Verkhoyansk, a town in northeast Russia about 260 miles south of the Arctic coast and about six miles north of the Arctic Circle, topped out at 100.4 Fahrenheit. The extreme temp was confirmed by the Russian Federal Service for Hydrometeorological and Environmental Monitoring after an inquiry by the World Meteorological Organization. The temp topped the city's previous record set on July 25, 1988. The confirmed temp may also have been the hottest temperature recorded north of the Arctic Circle, according to Etienne Kapikian, a meteorologist with Meteo France. To put the extreme in context, Siberia, one of the world's coldest places in winter, reached 100F in 2020 before Dallas or Houston did. The average high in late June in Verkhoyansk is only in the upper 60s.

June 21

America's New England region was feeling the heat, too, said NBC 10 Boston, with four consecutive days in the 90s in the Merrimack Valley, Southern New Hampshire and Champlain Valley. Boston and Providence got their first 90-degree day of the season yesterday, too.

It seemed appropriate that the only solar eclipse for the year should be nicknamed the "Ring of Fire". Space.com said the sight dazzled skywatchers across Africa and Asia. During this type of solar spectacle, the moon covers most of the sun, leaving a corona around its perimeter at the full moment of eclipse. While most eclipse seasons typically have two eclipses — one lunar and one solar — 2020 had three. This solar eclipse was the second of that trio. The first, a lunar eclipse, happened on June 5. The final of the three, another lunar eclipse, was set to happen late on the night of July 4-5. The lunar eclipses were of the penumbral type — very slight and not as flashy as, say, the "Ring of Fire".

June 23

That girl was shakin', snappin' her fingers — a powerful earthquake, that is, that struck Mexico, according to The Associated Press. Centered near the southern Mexico resort of Huatulco, the quake, sadly, killed at least two people, swayed buildings in Mexico City and sent thousands fleeing into the streets. Mexico President Andrés Manuel López Obrador said one person was killed and another injured in a building collapse in Huatulco. Otherwise he said reports were of minor damage from the magnitude 7.4 quake, including broken windows and collapsed walls. Oaxaca Gov. Alejandro Murat later said a second person was killed in an apparent house collapse in the tiny mountain village of San Juan Ozolotepec. The state-run oil company, known as Pemex, said the quake caused a fire at its refinery in the Pacific coast city of Salina Cruz, relatively near the epicenter. It said one worker was injured and the flames were quickly extinguished.

President Obrador said there had been more than 140 aftershocks, most of them small. Seismic alarms sounded midmorning with enough warning for residents to exit buildings. Power was knocked out to some areas. Helicopters flew over downtown Mexico City and police patrols sounded their sirens. Groups of people still milled around in close proximity on streets and sidewalks in some neighborhoods of the capital about an hour after the quake. Inside a Mexico City military barracks converted to a Covid-19 hospital, medical staff suited in protective equipment tried to calm anxious patients. Unable to evacuate to isolation areas, patients huddled under a large beam in the women's ward while a nurse tried to calm one having a panic attack. From her hospital bed where she lay connected to oxygen, patient Teresa Juárez could only wish for the event to pass quickly. Diabetic and with high blood pressure, Juárez said she thought about her five children. "It's horrible. You're here and you don't know what to do," she said.

June 24

AGGRESSIVE HUMAN BITING TICKS INVADING CONNECTICUT, shouted KICKS 105.5 Radio. "Just when you thought 2020 couldn't get any worse, human biting ticks have infiltrated into Connecticut, specifically Fairfield County. What a year it's been. We're only halfway through 2020 and we've already experienced a pandemic, massive protests, riots, civil unrest, and now how about throwing some human biting ticks in the mix?!" *Aggressive* human biting ticks, at that, responsible for an array of diseases.

The gnarly beast was identified as the "Lone Star" tick. According to the Connecticut Agricultural Experiment Station, the tick is usually found in the southeastern part of the United States, but was expanding its territory and starting to infiltrate parts of the Northeast. Now the CAES had documented cases in Fairfield and New Haven Counties, two areas that hadn't had *any* previous record of activity for this specific species of tick.

The Lone Star tick's bite was said to be extremely irritating. This species also had a history of spreading diseases like tularemia, ehrlichiosis, rickettsiosis, Heartland virus disease, southern tick-associated rash illness, red meat allergy and, likely, a newly identified Bourbon virus disease.

Dr. Goudarz Molaei, a research scientist in charge of the CAES Tick Surveillance and Testing Program, had been monitoring the Lone Star tick's migration over the last decade and theorized why we were seeing them now in areas where they had never appeared before. "Rising global temperatures, ecologic changes, reforestation, and increases in commerce and travel are important underlying factors influencing the rate and extent of range expansion for ticks and associated disease-causing pathogens. It is anticipated that warming temperatures associated with climate change may lead to the continued geographic range expansion and abundance of this tick, increasing its importance as an emerging threat to humans, domesticated animals and wildlife."

On another topic and given Siberia's recent extreme heat report and other global heatwave alerts, National Geographic pondered, "Why so hot so early in the summer?" Axial tilt had much to do with it, NG proposed. "Earth is kind of like a ball spinning on an invisible stick (its axis) while it orbits around the sun. That stick is not aligned straight up and down with respect to the sun though, and is instead tilted just a bit. When the planet's orbit causes its axis to tilt closest to the sun, we get our longest day of the year, which we call the summer solstice. The Northern Hemisphere had just passed that sunny marker. While there are many of us that enjoy basking in the heat, there's heat, then there's *heat*. Like the unusual kind of heat that was hitting Russia," NG noted. "Average temperatures in the high Arctic have been climbing quickly. Since December, air temperatures in the Russian Arctic have been nearly 11F higher than the average seen over the past four decades. If warming continues unabated, records like the one set in Verkhoyansk are just the tip of a rapidly melting iceberg."

June 28

A dust plume bigger than Texas crashed into the U.S., observed Space.com. Originating in the Sahara Desert, the dust drifted across the Atlantic Ocean. This type of thing had happened before, according to Marshall Shepherd, director of the University of Georgia's Atmospheric Sciences Program. Hundreds of millions of tons of dust from the giant North African desert collect in plumes and move west every year, and those plumes have long helped build up Caribbean beaches and fertilize soil in the Amazon, Shepherd said. The dust also routinely posed respiratory issues for people in impacted areas.

However, this plume, which the National Weather Service (NWS) forecast would blanket the U.S. Southeast and Puerto Rico, was the biggest in at least the past 50 years. The dust outbreak was "by far the most extreme of the MODIS satellite record — our most detailed, continuous record of global dust back to 2002," Michael Lowry, an atmospheric scientist at the Federal Emergency Management Agency (FEMA), stated in a Tweet. MODIS (the Moderate Resolution Imaging Spectroradiometer) is a NOAA satellite instrument that takes daily pictures of the Earth to track weather events.

June 29

Like a scene out of "JAWS", a shark showed up at Rockaway Beach days before NYC beachgoers were given a pandemic green light to go back in the water there, said the New York Post. A local resident, Regina Cantoni, was near Beach 100 mid-afternoon when she spotted a fin in the clear waters, just 10 to 15 feet from where she was sitting on the sand. Hundreds of beachgoers waved off social distancing protocols as they swarmed toward the big fish, she said. "The whole beach came to the shore … and started screaming, 'Shark!'" she told The Post. The 43-year-old real estate agent followed the fin east, where at one point, the shark seemed to be letting itself wash up on shore with the tide. "It looked hurt because I could spot some blood on the body," Cantoni said. Photos posted on Twitter by the Rockaway Times showed the approximately seven-foot sea creature on the sand, splattered in blood. The Parks Department said the thresher shark was injured after getting caught on a jetty at Beach 86, and later died. The city's 14 miles of beaches had been open to sunbathers prior to the shark sighting, but due to coronavirus restrictions, swimming had been prohibited.

Cape Cod officials were seeing fins near their shores, too, said FOX 61. Officials were reminding visitors ahead of the July Fourth holiday that the area remained a popular getaway for other summertime travelers: great white sharks. Cape Cod National Seashore Chief Ranger Leslie Reynolds warned that the predators were coming close enough to shore to be a concern for swimmers. Officials in Orleans, Mass., also documented at least two shark attacks on seals in recent days. And Greg Skomal, a prominent shark scientist with the state Division of Marine Fisheries, said he tagged three great whites circling a whale carcass earlier this month as his research team began its work for the season.

June 30

Northern Russia continued to set heat records, according to Weather. com. Ust'-Olenek soared to 93.7F (typically, high temperatures there are only around 50-54F). This town on Russia's Arctic coast, about 2,500 miles northeast of Moscow and over 400 miles north of the Arctic Circle, in fact, may have registered the farthest north Arctic 90-degree temperature on record, according to an analysis by Alaska-based climatologist Brian Brettschneider.

This wasn't just a June story. Berkeley Earth lead scientist Robert Rohde noted that Russia destroyed its record warmest January-May period in 2020 by a whopping 35F over the previous record warmest first five months of a year, logged in 2016. The persistent warm and dry weather fueled wildfires which had already begun scorching parts of northern Russia in April and continued to burn into June.

Ok, no one leave the room, a star is missing. Science Alert reported a massive star had disappeared from a distant galaxy — and no one was sure where it went. "Massive stars aren't like your car keys. They're not going to disappear under a pile of mail on your kitchen counter, or end up in the washing machine. But a massive star that astronomers were observing for a decade now appears to be totally missing," SA mused. In the very late stages of its lifespan and located in a dwarf galaxy called PHL 293B (75 million light years away), the star was shining brightly between 2001 and 2011, when different teams of astronomers were regularly observing it to obtain more information on how stars end their lives. But in observations obtained in 2019, the star's signature was completely absent.

The mystery deepened, said SA. When researchers looked back through archival data from 2011 and 2016, looking for some clue as to the star's disappearance, its light was present in the former, but missing in the latter. Somehow, after 2011, the star vanished without a trace.

And there was a really exciting possibility that the star collapsed down into a black hole, without the supernova flash that had previously been thought to be a necessary component of such an event. "If true," said astrophysicist Andrew Allan of Trinity College Dublin in Ireland, "this would be the first direct detection of such a monster star ending its life in this manner."

July 1

Looking back at May and June, Weather.com noted that these two most tornado-prone months experienced the *fewest* tornadoes since the

1950s. "Over the last 20 years, May (272) and June (202) have averaged the most tornadoes in the U.S., but 2020 ripped up that script.

Only 59 tornadoes were estimated by NOAA's Storm Prediction Center in May, the fewest in any May since at least since 1970, possibly since the 1950s. The tornado swoon continued in June, with only 50 tornadoes estimated by the SPC, fewest since the early 1950s."

The monthly tallies were more on par with an average October or November, instead of two months notorious for destructive tornadoes and outbreaks. Only three of those tornadoes – two in May and one in June — were rated at least EF2, both record-low stronger tornado totals for each month. What was also remarkable was the lack of tornadoes in parts of the most tornado-prone Plains states of Oklahoma and Kansas — not just in May or June, but also year-to-date. An explanation? A pair of weather patterns largely unfavorable for tornado-spawning severe thunderstorms were in place in May 2020. A generally unfavorable pattern for tornadoes with persistent high pressure over the nation's mid-section characterized June as well.

Weather.com also looked back at the first half of the year, with regard to South Florida and remarkable records being set there. "Florida warmth may not sound weird, but persistent heat crushed records in the first half of 2020. It kicked into high gear with the state's record hottest and second driest March, since 1895. On one mid-April day, Miami failed to drop below 80 degrees for the first time on record in April," Weather said.

It only grew more miserable in June. National Hurricane Center meteorologist Eric Blake noted that Miami had its hottest week on record in late June. In the last 10 days of the month, the temp dipped below 80 degrees only once, on the morning after Father's Day. Miami ended June by tying its second hottest all-time temperature of 98 degrees.

It had been the warmest first half of any year on record not only in Miami, but also in Fort Myers, Orlando and West Palm Beach, according to the Southeast Regional Climate Center. Taken together, Miami, Fort Lauderdale and Key West set over 120 combined daily warm records in the first half of 2020, according to NBC6 Miami Chief Meteorologist John Morales.

July 3

"Jellyfish the size of dinner plates," was the cry from Eyewitness News 3. The beefy jellies were the welcoming committee for visitors to beaches in the Northeast United States over the Fourth of July weekend. The Lion's Mane jellyfish, which can be up to four feet in diameter and have tentacles over a hundred feet long, had been spotted from Maine to Massachusetts. "The ones that we're seeing here are probably not much bigger than maybe a dinner plate," said Steve Spina, Assistant Curator of Fishes at the New England Aquarium, "which is big enough."

Because of their size, these jellyfish are particularly dangerous to swimmers. Their long tentacles can sting a person whose guard is down because the fish looks like it's feet away.

"The abundance of them this year is what's unusual. There's an awful lot," said Spina.

The Lion's Mane jellyfish is the world's largest jellyfish, the news station shared. It can be found in the North Atlantic and Pacific oceans' colder waters, but has been gradually spreading south. Theresa Keil of The National Aquarium shared, "The jellyfish frequently appear in deep water in the North Atlantic in late spring and early summer. But this year, they're washing up on shore later — and in more significant numbers — than before."

July 6

Nothing to see here, just the Bubonic Plague, according to Forbes, with regard to a warning issued about the centuries-old disease's detection in China's Inner Mongolia. "There's a suspected case of the bubonic plague in Bayan Nur, a city in the Chinese region of Inner Mongolia," reported Forbes. "Yes, this is *the* plague that's caused by the bacteria *Yersinia pestis,* which can be transmitted to humans after fleas bite infected rodents. Yes, that's fleas biting animals like rats, mice, and marmots. Yes, fleas biting rats is not a pretty picture. Yes, *Yersinia pestis* is also what caused the 'Black Death' that killed over 50 million people in Europe in the mid-1300s. Yes, there were four other cases of the plague in Inner Mongolia just last November."

Officials in Bayan Nur issued a third-level alert, which "forbids the hunting and eating of animals that could carry plague and asks the public to report any suspected cases of plague or fever with no clear causes, and to report any sick or dead marmots." The alert was not a more high level one as there are now antibiotics such as streptomycin, gentamicin, doxycycline and ciprofloxacin that can readily treat the plague, assuming they are administered in time. Apparently, the disease appears from time to time still, on *all* continents. In the U.S., since 2000, for example, there have been an average of seven reported human plague cases each year. The highest tally was 17 in 2006. Most of these cases occurred in the West and Southwest portions of the U.S. Still… it's… the… Bubonic Plague… Sheesh.

July 11

"Are We Ready for Disease X?" OZY queried, stating that there are 1.67 million overall unknown viruses floating around and that global fissures have made it hard to discover the one that will attack next. "As the world grapples with a health crisis that still hasn't peaked, researchers, governments and global agencies like the WHO are scrambling to prepare for the next pandemic. It's a daunting challenge," OZY stated.

Growing mistrust between nations has increased the risk of the spread of a pathogen — that might otherwise be stopped — from turning into the next global killer virus. The diagnosis of a sick herdsman in China's Inner Mongolia region last week had sent the world into a tizzy. He had the Bubonic Plague, as we had learned. Informed of the case, the World Health Organization (WHO) said, "At the moment, we are not considering it high risk, but we're watching it, monitoring it carefully."

OZY suggested that "overwhelming caution over a centuries-old disease betrays a deeper unease that's undermining the medical fraternity, governments and global agencies such as the WHO. The coronavirus curve is far from flattened — more than 550,000 people have died, and cases are rising rapidly in the United States, Brazil and India, the three worst-affected nations. But researchers are already beginning to focus on what the next pandemic might look like and how to fight it."

OZY related that, in late June, scientists announced they had discovered a new strain of the H1N1 flu strain spreading among pig farm workers in China, and cautioned it could turn into a pandemic unless controlled. In the past week, the Chinese Embassy in Kazakhstan warned its nationals about an "unknown pneumonia" with a higher fatality rate than Covid-19 spreading there.

Dr. Krutika Kuppalli, an infectious diseases expert, vice chair of the IDSA Global Health Committee, and biosecurity fellow at the Johns Hopkins Center for Health Security, said the past 40 years have seen a fourfold increase in the number of emerging pathogens that have led to major outbreaks — SARS, H1N1, MERS, Nipah, Zika and Ebola among them. Of the 1.67 million unknown viruses in the world, an estimated 827,000 had the capacity to infect humans.

One key reason for our growing vulnerability to these diseases, Pulitzer-winning author Laurie Garrett proffered in her book, *The Coming Plague*, was humankind's "complacency born of proud discoveries and medical triumphs," which leaves us "unprepared for the coming plague."

July 12

CNN reported that the United States had hit its 10th billion-dollar weather disaster earlier than any other year, making 2020 the sixth consecutive year with at least 10 extreme weather events — also a record, according to the National Oceanic and Atmospheric Administration (NOAA). The 10 storms had tormented the US with tornadoes, damaging winds and hail. Seven of the 10 storms occurred in the South or Southeast, including three tornado outbreaks. The Easter Sunday outbreak alone saw 190 tornadoes tear across the region, killing 36 people.

Adam Smith, a climatologist at NOAA, forecast that "Americans might see more severe storms this year than ever before. Since 1980, the US has averaged close to seven billion-dollar weather disasters annually. But the last five years have seen nearly 14 severe storms on average. There will be more this year if the current pace continues."

July 14

A squirrel in Morrison, Colorado, tested positive for the Bubonic Plague, bringing Inner Mongolia's nightmare scenario right to our own backyard, reported CBS News.

July 15

NBC Connecticut issued a First Alert about a heat wave forthcoming in the state, with temps expected to surge into the low to middle 90s over four consecutive days. The news service anticipated posting Heat Advisories for parts of the state when heat index values would make it feel like nearly 100 degrees.

July 20

Researchers released a report of the discovery of a "sea cockroach" species in Indonesia and it was pure nightmare fuel, said Mashable SE Asia. "In a 2018 expedition to survey uncharted waters off the southern coast of West Java, a team of researchers made some very peculiar findings, including that of a just-identified new species, Bathynomus raksasa, a giant isopod, which usually can be found scavenging off the remains of dead marine animals at the bottom of the ocean. Giant isopods are often called 'sea cockroaches' because they bear a striking resemblance to the pests we have above the sea, lurking in the walls of our homes and the sewage systems of our cities. They come in all shapes and sizes, growing to an average of 13 inches. But there are some that can even grow up to 20 inches, of which this new discovery by LKCNHM is a part of," Mashable related.

Fittingly-named, the giant isopod can apparently survive for long periods of time without food, just like their cockroach brethren. According to the Natural History Museum of London, the size of the giant isopod is attributed to the lack of natural predators in their deep-sea habitat, allowing them to grow larger than one would normally expect of other sea creatures. The museum also noted that they have less meat than crabs, which makes them less appealing for any predators that do swing by.

July 21

Bunny Ebola. Good God. Popular Science said a deadly virus was spreading with alarming speed amongst wild and domestic rabbits in seven southwestern U.S. states. The contagion causes an illness called rabbit hemorrhagic disease that had earned the nickname "Bunny Ebola" because the disease causes massive internal bleeding and bloody discharge around the nose and mouth. The virus kills swiftly — as happened in February, when pet rabbits boarding at a veterinary practice in Manhattan suddenly began to die without warning, said PS.

The disease is deeply worrying for domestic rabbit owners and was likely to have consequences for wild rabbit, hare and pika populations. An outbreak last year in northwestern Washington state had devastating impacts on both feral and pet rabbits. Animal health officials have been anxiously tracking its spread and trying to protect the most endangered rabbits from the disease, which is very contagious and has a high mortality rate.

"They both represent a longtime fear that has come true," says Susan Kerr, an education and outreach specialist at the Washington State Department of Agriculture. Public health officials have worried about a pandemic, while rabbit owners have watched the virus spread across Europe for years. "Rabbit enthusiasts have always been terrified of this disease."

Rabbit hemorrhagic disease was first recognized in China in 1984, said PS. It is caused by several pathogens that belong to a family called caliciviruses, which are unrelated to the ones that cause Ebola. In 2010, a new version of the disease arose in France, spread among domestic and wild rabbits, and eventually traveled as far as Australia. Known as rabbit hemorrhagic disease virus 2 (RHDV2), it can kill infected rabbits within a few days by causing widespread inflammation, problems with blood clotting and bleeding, and organ failure. "The organs can't do their functions anymore because there is so much blood in them," Kerr said.

Meanwhile, in the Indian state of Assam, tens of thousands of people had been displaced as floods heaped misery on the pandemic-stricken region, said CNN. "Unrelenting monsoon rains have triggered severe flooding, killing at least 85 people, displacing tens of thousands of residents and drowning rare wildlife in a national park," CNN noted.

Since May, raging floodwaters had inundated thousands of villages on the banks of the overflowing Brahmaputra river, forcing more than 145,648 people out of their homes and hampering efforts to prevent the continued spread of the coronavirus. The most recent impact reports shared that 48,197 displaced residents were taking shelter at 276 relief camps set up across the state, while others had returned home after the flood receded in their regions, according to the Assam State Disaster Management Authority.

Famous for its tea plantations, the northeastern state is hit by floods and landslides every year during the monsoon season. But this year's deluge arrived as the country was struggling to contain the spread of the coronavirus. India had recorded more than one million confirmed cases to this point — the third highest in the world after the U.S. and Brazil.

The virus was spreading rapidly in Assam, infecting more than 1,000 people every day over the past week. In total, the state of about 25 million people had reported over 25,000 cases, including 58 deaths. The deluge, in the meantime, had affected more than 2.4 million people in 24 of the 33 districts in Assam. It had also swamped large swaths of a national park, killing over 100 wild animals, including a dozen rhinos.

July 22

A tornado, but with fire, #because2020. FOX News reported that a "firenado" had been spotted amidst an explosive northeastern California wildfire that had already scorched more than 9,000 acres. Known as the "Hog Fire" and burning in Lassen County west of Susanville, the blaze was forcing firefighters to take suppressive action and construct fire containment lines, according to Cal Fire. At one point, it created its own weather, generating lightning, thunder, rain and "fire whirls" out of a huge ash plume towering above.

Wendell Hohmann, an NWS forecaster who first observed the firenado, said that it was the first time, to his knowledge, that there had been a tornado warning of this nature. "It's probably the first time it's been issued outside of a thunderstorm environment," Hohmann said. Winds hit 60 mph in the area, whipping up the cloud, which posed an extremely dangerous situation for firefighters.

Two thousand miles to the northwest, a powerful earthquake, registering 7.8 on the Richter scale, struck Alaska, said Tri-State Weather. It spurred a Tsunami Warning, warning sirens, helicopters aloft to wake people up, and a coastal evacuation.

July 27

What? More sharks? News 12 Long Island (New York) shared, "Two shark sightings close beaches along Nassau's South Shore". The first sighting was at Lido Beach, by a lifeguard patrolling in the water. "It came out, shot out of the water, spun around and it didn't look like a dolphin, it was definitely a shark," said the lifeguard. The second sighting was in Long Beach. The water was subsequently shut down to swimmers, all the way from Atlantic Beach to Jones Beach. Officials ventured that the shark in Lido was a bull shark, approximately seven to 10 feet long, swimming about eight to 10 feet from shore. Lifeguards had been on high alert since earlier in the week after a ray was discovered with "sizable" chunks bitten out of it.

Tragically, one of these beasts apparently killed a woman in Maine, of all places, said NBC CT. "A witness said the woman was swimming 'when she was injured in what appeared to be a shark attack,'" according to a statement from the Maine Department of Marine Resources. Kayakers in the area — Bailey Island, in Harpswell, in the southeastern part of the state — took her to shore, where paramedics were called. But she was pronounced dead by first responders almost immediately after.

People renting and living in the area said this type of gruesome attack was so unusual and so shocking in Maine that some people wouldn't be getting back in the water for a while. Swimmers were being advised to be cautious and not to swim near seals or large groups of fish. Prior to this incident, there had been just one shark attack documented in Maine since 1837, according to the International Shark Attack File maintained by the Florida Museum of Natural History and the University of Florida.

July 28

NBC2 News gave an early heads-up through Twitter about a storm it was monitoring: "TRACKING NOW - Tropical Storm Isaias is likely to develop as early as today and head for the Leeward Islands where Tropical Storm Warnings are in place."

Meanwhile, above us, an asteroid the size of a car had just zipped by Earth in a close flyby, said Space.com. The rock passed our planet at a range that rivaled the orbits of some high-flying satellites. Labeled asteroid 2020 OY4, the mass was first detected on July 26. It made its closest approach today, zipping by our planet at a speed of about 27,700 mph, according to the European Space Agency. Though the asteroid was just under 10 feet wide, it posed no impact risk to Earth, but did approach the flight paths of geosynchronous satellites.

August 2

Sharks were in the news again. WCBS NewsRadio 880 announced, "Bull Sharks Are Making a Comeback". An expert in the field speculated that there were two main reasons for the sharks' return: warm weather and the presence of more bait fish near the shoreline. Beaches had been going through a purification process, with fewer swimmers and boats in the water for months because of the pandemic. "But with that comes some other caveats, and one of them is more aquatic life and more of the feeders that draw these sharks in," the expert said. Supporting his conjecture: there had been 14 shark sightings in Hempstead, Long Island (NY) in the past week, with beaches closing again after multiple sharks were spotted. The town added extra lifeguards on surfboards and jet skis to help keep a lookout and beachgoers safe.

On the opposite side of the country, a Southern California wildfire had forced thousands to evacuate, said NBC News. Known as the "Apple Fire", the blaze quickly spread across 12,000 acres, destroying at least one home and two structures and forcing 7,800 people in all to evacuate. Centered in Riverside County, about 75 miles east of Los Angeles, the fire was being fought by 375 firefighters with dozens of fire engines and air support. But it remained entirely uncontained. As it moved north into San

Bernardino County, evacuation orders were issued for two areas, Potato Canyon and Oak Glen, the California Department of Forestry and Fire Protection said. Mandatory evacuations were applied to more than 2,500 homes and about 7,800 residents, said CalFire spokesman Rob Roseen. Firefighters worked in scorching heat that reached 107 degrees, according to the National Weather Service. About an hour southwest, in Coachella Valley, temperatures hit 120 degrees, said NBC News.

August 3

Tropical Storm Isaias began to get on our own figurative radar in Fairfield, Connecticut. Fairfield HamletHub shared, "Tropical Storm Warning in effect for Fairfield County, CT and surrounding coastal regions. We should be feeling the storm's impacts by late afternoon, Tuesday, Aug. 4. Prepare accordingly."

The National Weather Service echoed the alert for the Fairfield, CT area, indicating, "Tropical storm conditions possible. Showers and possibly a thunderstorm. Some of the storms could produce heavy rainfall. High near 78. Chance of precipitation is 80%. New rainfall amounts between three quarters and one inch possible."

August 4

WHOMP. Tropical Storm Isaias hit our Fairfield, CT area and southwestern Connecticut shore *hard*, much to the surprise of local residents and even the weather services. Westport, CT's Patch news service confirmed, in fact, "Westport Was Hit By A Tornado, NWS Says". Patch said, "Tuesday's storm left Westport in a shambles, with nearly 300 roads at one point closed due to downed trees and wires. And now we know why, Westport was hit by a tornado. The National Weather Service on Friday confirmed that a tornado swept through town, packing winds of between 95 and 105 mph. It touched down at about 1:40 p.m. on Tuesday (Aug. 4), and measured 25 yards wide and 50 yards long, according to the weather service."

The NWS described: "A discreet, low-topped storm cell, moving north-northwest from Long Island Sound and over Saugatuck Shores in Westport CT, produced a waterspout that made landfall as an EF1 tornado. The waterspout was captured on video by a private meteorologist. The tornado produced severe damage to a house on Surf Rd., with the roof being ripped off, as well as portions of the second floor's supporting wall structure. This debris was tossed about 30-50 feet north on the property. In addition, the tops of several pine trees in the front and side yard were either sheared or snapped off. The tornado likely quickly lifted and possibly tracked north as a funnel cloud for another 1 to 2 miles, before dissipating. The funnel cloud could have touched down as a waterspout on the Saugatuck River, south of Route 1, based on an eyewitness report from S. Compo Road in Westport, CT. Otherwise, downstream damage reports are inconclusive for tornado damage, but consistent with the damaging 40 to 50 mph straight line sustained winds and 60 to 70 mph gusts observed between 2pm and 5pm across southwestern CT from Tropical Storm Isaias."

According to NBC Connecticut's Chief Meteorologist Ryan Hanrahan, the remarkable twister was the "first tornado on record in Connecticut associated with a tropical storm or hurricane."

Isaias was, indeed, a surprising bully, leaving five dead along the East Coast in all as it made its way to Canada, said CNN. In New York, Mario Siles, 60, was found inside a van "with trauma about the head and body," a New York Police Department spokeswoman said, and pronounced dead at the scene. An 83-year-old woman in Delaware was found under a large branch in a pond near her home, reported Delaware State Police. In St. Mary's County in southern Maryland, the driver of a car died after a tree fell on the vehicle's roof. Earlier, at least two people were killed when a tornado struck a mobile home park in Windsor, North Carolina, Bertie County officials said. Twelve people there were also injured and taken to hospitals. A resident of the neighborhood said she hid in her bathroom with her two sons. "We didn't have a lot of time to react once it finally hit. I mean, it hit all at once," she said. "For lack of a better word, it was hell. You don't really think about anything else but just holding the kids and hoping it doesn't tear the house up." Onsite at the trailer park, local Sheriff John Holley observed, "It's bad. It doesn't look real. It looks like something on TV. Nothing is there." There were preliminary reports of more than 30 tornadoes spurred by Isaias along the East Coast.

August 5

Our Fairfield, CT area really got socked by Isais. Fairfield Police Department provided a STORM UPDATE: "As of 8:45 AM, United Illuminating (the dominant local electricity provider) is reporting that 12,300 (50.78%) Fairfield customers are without power. There are numerous downed trees and wires still in the roadway. Please treat every wire as if it was live. UI has not provided any timeline for global restorations at this time due to the amount of damage in Town. The Emergency Management team will be speaking with UI this morning with the hope of gaining a better idea of when we can expect power to be restored. We are all just as frustrated as you are but, please, be patient...damage is significant."

The FPD stressed to residents, "Use caution while driving as many traffic signals/lights are not operational due to power outages. Stop in all directions at intersections with traffic lights that are not functioning. Stay home if possible to allow crews to safely clear roadways of debris. Many people are using portable generators to power their homes. Please make sure that generators are only run OUTSIDE. Please make sure your generator is vented properly and away from your home to prevent a deadly carbon monoxide build-up. Emergency Management crews will be working all day assessing the damage to the Town. DPW has worked through the night to clear and open roads and will continue their efforts today. Many people have sustained major damage to their homes due to falling trees. Building Department officials will be out today assessing structural damage."

With regard to the rest of Connecticut, NBC CT shared that more than 600,000 people were without power and said "clean up from this storm will not happen overnight."

FOX News weighed in to add that Tropical Storm Isaias caused the "second-largest outage in Con Edison history," according to the company. The utility said that the storm's rampage through the New York City area shoved trees and branches onto power lines, bringing down equipment that left 257,000 customers without power. "The destruction surpassed Hurricane Irene, which caused 204,000 customer outages in August 2011," the company said in a news release. According to ConEd, the record for storm-related outages was 1.1 million caused by Hurricane Sandy in October 2012 and a Nor'easter that followed the storm. The company said that service had already been restored to more than 48,000 customers, but it was clear that restoration for all would take "multiple days".

FOX News also shared that Tropical Storm Isaias caused a 147 mph wind gust atop Mount Washington in New Hampshire, as the storm roared northward, monitored by the National Weather Service. "This is the highest wind gust reported there in the month of August," the forecast office said. The Mount Washington Observatory said on Facebook that the storm knocked out the main and secondary internet service. Workers were still able to put up brief posts mid-storm using a "single bar of service", sharing that winds were "moving back down."

August 6

Town of Fairfield, CT First Selectwoman Brenda Kupchick offered a Tropical Storm Isaias recovery update: "The Emergency Management Team and I continue to work with UI. We received a new liaison this morning and I look forward to better coordination going forward. Our DPW crews continue to work on clearing trees and brush that are not connected to power lines."

The Fairfield Police Department trumpeted, "Water, WiFi and Power! We are deploying our mobile command post to the Old Navy parking lot to provide bottled water, WiFI internet and power for charging electronics. The command post will be staffed from 7a-11p to provide these resources. Please see uniformed personnel at the vehicle for assistance."

WTNH (CT) weighed in with the human toll, for Connecticut, from Isaias. "Governor Ned Lamont reported two Connecticut residents have died and five were injured; the five injured have severe injuries. One of the deaths reported was that of a 66-year-old man in Naugatuck who had gotten out of his vehicle to clear branches from the road and was struck by a falling tree at the height of the storm. Newtown Police reported that Stephen Caciopoli, 33, of Newtown, died in a masonry saw accident while helping a friend cut some downed trees from the storm. He was taken to Danbury Hospital where he was pronounced dead."

Amidst our local misery, CBS News chimed in with a longer-term hurricane forecast from weather experts. "The 2020 Atlantic hurricane season is racking up storms at breakneck speed. To date, the season is about two weeks ahead of record pace and it's only one-third of the way through. The news has become more concerning as the research team at Colorado State University (CSU) — the standard bearer for seasonal forecasts — released the most dire forecast in their 37-year history. Labeling the 2020 hurricane season 'extremely active', the team is now predicting 24 named storms, including 12 total hurricanes and five major hurricanes — each figure about double that of a normal season. If the forecast proves accurate, 2020 would be the second most active Atlantic hurricane season, behind only the record-shattering 2005 season which brought Hurricanes Katrina and Wilma."

The CSU team explained, "Only 21 storm names are allotted each year because the letters Q, U, X, Y and Z are not used. As a result, if 24 tropical storms are indeed named, the National Hurricane Center will have to employ the Greek alphabet for overflow. This has only happened one time on record — in 2005 when the Atlantic experienced 28 named storms."

In addition, CSU suggested there was a 75% chance that the U.S. coast would be struck by a major hurricane — Category 3 or greater — during the 2020 season. This was significant as damage increases exponentially with wind speed. Category 3, 4 and 5 systems cause 85% of all hurricane damage, CBS noted.

Echoing the CSU team's dire predictions, the National Oceanic and Atmospheric Administration (NOAA) upgraded its hurricane forecast as well, shared CBS. NOAA's updated outlook called for 19 to 25 named storms, of which they said seven to 11 would become hurricanes, including three to six major hurricanes.

"This is one of the most active seasonal forecasts that NOAA has produced in its 22-year history of hurricane outlooks," said U.S. Secretary of Commerce Wilbur Ross, whose department oversees NOAA. "We encourage all Americans to do their part by getting prepared, remaining vigilant, and being ready to take action when necessary."

While CBS News pondered hurricanes, it also raised a question about heat waves, wondering if we should name them, like we do major storms. "If asked to recall a hurricane, odds are you'd immediately invoke memorable names like Sandy, Katrina or Harvey. You'd probably even remember something specific about the impact of the storm. But if asked to recall a heat wave, a vague recollection that it was hot during your last summer vacation may be about as specific as you can get," CBS mused.

Although heat waves rarely get the attention that hurricanes do, they kill far more people per year in the U.S. — about three times as many, according to the NOAA. For example, in 1995, a scorching heat wave in Chicago left 739 people dead, CBS said.

Heat waves are even more impactful overseas, partly because people there are less likely to have air conditioning. The European heat wave of 2003 is estimated to have caused an astounding 70,000 deaths, CBS said. In 2010, 56,000 people died from a heat wave in Russia.

CBS suggested that, perhaps if heat waves received as much public attention as hurricanes, lives could be saved. That was the idea behind a newly launched initiative that aimed to tackle the notoriety issue by naming and ranking heat waves. The hope was that, by raising awareness of the dangers, people would be more adequately prepared when heat waves struck. The initiative was being led by the Atlantic Council's Adrienne Arsht-Rockefeller Foundation Resilience Center (AARFRC). They, along with 30 global partners — including the cities of Miami, Mexico City, and Athens, Greece — announced the formation of the Extreme Heat Resilience Alliance. "This extreme heat crisis can no longer be the 'silent killer' it is," said Kathy Baughman McLeod, director of the AARFRC. "This growing risk — and related solutions — must be blasted from a megaphone to decision makers and to people everywhere."

August 7

Fairfield, CT's post-Isais woes continued. First Selectwoman Kupchick checked in with another Storm Update: "It has been a difficult week for our community that left many of us without electricity, access to internet or cable, including myself. I know you are frustrated with the response from UI; I am, too. One of the things that has added to my frustration is that, during previous storms, UI was able to provide a daily list of streets or target areas they would be working on to give residents an idea of when their power would be back on."

FS Kupchick offered a ray of hope: "I've had numerous command staff meetings with our Emergency Management Team that included working with the UI representative assigned to our town. Those meetings resulted in increased UI presence in our community. This morning, I had another conference call with our liaison at UI and pressed for more crews. I'm happy to report that an additional 10 crews were dispatched to the Hawthorne Substation where the National Guard is also assisting."

NBC CT vocalized local leaders' frustration with the response from utilities, in particular, Eversource, headlining, "'Shame on You Eversource': Conn. Leaders Sound Off as Hundreds of Thousands Remain Without Power". The recovery status was there for all to see: Nearly 330,000 Connecticut customers remained without electricity. Gov. Lamont had declared a state of emergency and received a presidential emergency declaration for Conn.

Eversource responded, estimating it would have power restored to most customers by late Tuesday night, a week after Tropical Storm Isaias hit the state, and that it would provide customers with restoration timelines.

August 8

Our Town of Fairfield, CT's First Selectwoman Kupchick offered her now-daily post-Isais update: "I met again this morning with the Emergency Management Team and representatives from UI to receive an update. Yesterday, Fairfield had 8,700 residents without power; this morning we have 5,351 still without power. In yesterday's update, I included information about the Hawthorne Substation located behind Sacred Heart University. Once repaired, this substation will power up a large amount of residents. UI is still working there and is reporting the damage was worse than they initially thought. The entire system needed to be reworked and UI brought in mutual aide crews for assistance. UI is estimating this substation, that has three large circuits, will be completed by midnight tonight."

While Fairfield was gradually getting back on its feet, Manitoba, one of Canada's westernmost provinces, had gotten knocked down. The Daily Mail reported, "A violent tornado wreaked havoc on farmland as it touched down, killing two teenagers and injuring another man. Incredible video and images from storm chasers tracking its path showed the wave of destruction that followed as the storm formed into its dangerous spiral and tore across fields in Scarth, Manitoba. Surrounding property and machinery were torn asunder in what is claimed to be one of the strongest tornadoes people in the area have seen."

Rescue services were called after a 54-year-old man became trapped in a vehicle that was flipped over by the tornado. Two 18-year-olds were also killed, the Royal Canadian Mounted Police confirmed Saturday afternoon, in a separate vehicle close to where the man was trapped, said the DM. "It threw two different vehicles, one into the ditch. There were two occupants trapped in there plus there were downed power lines around the vehicle also, so that hampered the rescue operation," a storm chaser shared. "I would say about 200 yards from the field, it threw another vehicle into the ditch… Unfortunately, as it threw it into the field, its occupant was thrown from the vehicle." He added that a tornado of this scale was rare to see and that it was on land for between ten and 15 minutes.

August 9

Fairfield Patch weighed in with some post-Isais tallies, citing the Town of Fairfield, CT had more outage events than any other nearby town. "More than 90 percent of electric customers in Fairfield had power early Sunday. But five days after Tropical Storm Isaias brought widespread damage and outages to town, seven percent of customers were still in the dark," Patch shared.

"As of about 3:30 a.m., 1,787 United Illuminating Co. customers in Fairfield had no power, according to the company, an improvement compared to the 25 percent that had been powerless roughly 24 hours earlier. The number of customers experiencing an outage peaked above 60 percent in the wake of the storm before holding steady around 50 percent for about two days," Patch said.

WCBS 880 checked in with wider, regional post-Isaias tallies. "Tens of thousands of people are still without power across the New York Tri-State Region as the temps kick back up today, creating dangerous conditions particularly for the elderly, infirm and those working from home due to the pandemic (that other ever-present crisis we're battling)."

And while our region struggled to regain power, the USGS reported that a magnitude 5.1 earthquake struck near Sparta, North Carolina at 8:07 a.m. EDT. "Seismic instruments indicate the earthquake originated at a depth of about 2.3 miles. The USGS currently estimates there is a low likelihood of casualties or damage from this earthquake. The event was widely felt, with more than 80,000 'Did You Feel It?' reports submitted as of 1 p.m. EDT. Most reported weak to light shaking while those closest to the epicenter felt strong to very strong shaking."

With a day highlighted by residual power outages and southern earthquakes, Space.com threw into the mix a report of a "mysterious fast radio burst detected closer to Earth than ever before."

"Thirty thousand years ago, a dead star on the other side of the Milky Way belched out a powerful mixture of radio and X-ray energy. On April 28, 2020, that belch swept over Earth, triggering alarms at observatories around the world. The signal was there and gone in half a second, but that's all scientists needed to confirm they had detected something remarkable: the first ever 'fast radio burst' (FRB) to emanate from a known star within the Milky Way, according to a study published July 27 in The Astrophysical Journal Letters," Space said.

Since their discovery in 2007, FRBs have puzzled scientists. The bursts of powerful radio waves last only a few milliseconds at most, but generate more energy in that time than Earth's sun does in a century, Space remarked. Scientists have yet to pin down what causes these blasts, but they've proposed everything from colliding black holes to the pulse of alien starships as possible explanations. So far, every known FRB has originated from another galaxy, hundreds of millions of light years away.

This FRB was different, Space noted. Telescope observations suggested that the burst came from a known neutron star — the fast-spinning, compact core of a dead star, which packs a sun's-worth of mass into a city-sized ball — about 30,000 light years from Earth in the constellation Vulpecula. The stellar remnant fits into an even stranger class of star called a magnetar, named for its incredibly powerful magnetic field, capable of spitting out intense amounts of energy long after the star itself has died.

It now seemed that magnetars were almost certainly the source of at least some of the universe's many mysterious FRBs, the study authors wrote.

"We've never seen a burst of radio waves, resembling a fast radio burst, from a magnetar before," lead study author Sandro Mereghetti, of the National Institute for Astrophysics in Milan, Italy, stated. "This is the first ever observational connection between magnetars and fast radio bursts."

The magnetar, named SGR 1935+2154, was discovered in 2014 when scientists saw it emitting powerful bursts of gamma rays and X-rays at random intervals. After quieting down for a while, the dead star woke up with a powerful X-ray blast in late April. Sandro and his colleagues detected this burst with the European Space Agency's (ESA) Integral satellite, designed to capture the most energetic phenomena in the universe. At the same time, a radio telescope in the mountains of British Columbia, Canada, detected a blast of radio waves coming from the same source. Radio telescopes in California and Utah confirmed the FRB the next day.

August 10

The National Weather Service informed us here in the New York Tri-State Region that it was going to be a scorcher today. A HEAT ADVISORY was issued, with the temp expected to reach 90F by 3pm, in the Fairfield/Bridgeport, CT area. Fairfield HamletHub relayed the news, with cautionary notes: STAY HYDRATED. SEEK SHADE. AVOID STRENUOUS ACTIVITY. DON'T LEAVE PETS OR KIDS UNATTENDED IN YOUR CAR.

August 11

"Itchy, stinging sea lice surface at Jersey Shore beaches" shared NJ.com. The news service ventured that, Tropical Storm Isaias, which hit New Jersey last week, likely pushed sea lice, normally abundant in southern waters off Florida, northward toward the Jersey Shore. Sea lice, the service informed, induce a skin reaction, called seabather's eruption, caused by the bites of the larvae when they become trapped in a person's bathing suit or clothing. The pressure from the fabric pushing against the sea lice triggers their stinging cells.

While Jersey swimmers were itching, USA Today was calling an alert to a new tropical depression forming in the Atlantic, though forecasters noted it would likely be short-lived. Dubbed Tropical Depression Eleven, the system had winds of 35 mph and was located about 1,450 miles east of the Lesser Antilles in the Caribbean. It was moving to the west at 16 mph. Weather watchers indicated that if its sustained winds reached 39 mph, the depression would become Tropical Storm Josephine. To date, the earliest Atlantic "J" storm on record was Jose, which formed Aug. 22, 2005.

In the Midwest, more than a million people were without power from severe storms there, while the heat kept broiling the Northeast, said ABC News. A bucking bronco derecho, like the American Southwest experienced back in early June, moved through the Midwest from Nebraska to Ohio initiating more than 500 damaging severe storm reports along with the extensive power outages. The highest winds in this derecho were in Linn County, Iowa, clocked at 112 mph. In Lee County, Illinois, winds gusted to 92 mph and, in Chicago's Lincoln Square, a weather observer recorded a wind gust to 85 mph.

Meanwhile, thousands of Northeasterners were still without power from Isaias, as a heatwave continued. Eight states, in fact, from New Jersey to Maine, were under Heat Advisories, with some areas expecting a real-feel of 95 to 102 degrees.

Way above Earth, the Perseid Meteor Shower was to peak after midnight, said NPR. "If you're tired of binge-watching TV during the pandemic, Mother Nature has an alternative. All you have to do is go outside between about 2 a.m. Wednesday and dawn local time, lie on your back and look up at the sky. The meteors and fireballs of the Perseid meteor shower should be streaking," NPR enticed.

NASA said it was going to be "one of the best" meteor shows of the year, primarily because of the sheer number of meteors (50 to 100 meteors per hour) as well as their fireballs — larger, brighter explosions of light and color that last longer than an average meteor streak. NASA added that summer temperatures make for ideal viewing conditions.

August 12

It was "fins up" again at New York beaches after a "sizable shark" was spotted, said the Hudson Valley Post. "Despite the heat, many beaches in New York are closed following 'red-flag' shark sightings," HVP said. "Town of Hempstead beaches (between Point Lookout and Lido West Town Park) are currently red-flagged (no swimming)," the Town posted to Twitter.

Nassau County Executive Laura Curran reported Nickerson Beach had been closed as well after a shark was sighted there. "A shark was just spotted 40 yards offshore by lifeguards and beachgoers. This is the 17th confirmed sighting in Nassau this summer," Curran tweeted.

Officials explained that, as water heats up, sharks are known to move closer to shore in search of food.

As Long Island beachgoers scrambled for safety, The Washington Post reported flash flooding in northern Virginia had caused a 50 x 100-foot sinkhole to open up in Manassas Park, forcing water rescues. One car was swept by floodwaters into a creek, and two other cars were "in danger of going into the sinkhole," Capt. Frank Winston of the Manassas Park Police said.

The U.K. was about to get soggy, too, amidst their own heatwave, said Sky News. Adverse weather warnings had been put in place for large parts of the country as it braced for thunderstorms and heavy rain amid soaring temperatures. A yellow thunderstorm warning had been issued for all of England and Wales by the Met Office, while eastern Scotland — between Edinburgh, Inverness and Aberdeen — had a more serious amber warning in place. The latter warning meant people would need to be on alert for flash flooding and damage to buildings from lightning strikes, torrential downpours and hailstones, as well as widespread disruption on the roads and to public transport, while deep and fast floodwater could be a threat to human life.

August 14

The U.K.'s rain misery equated on the grief scale to the wild West's fire woes, according to CNN. Hundreds of people had been evacuated after wildfires destroyed more than 90,000 acres across three states. Specifically, evacuation orders had been issued in areas threatened by the "Lake Fire" and "Ranch2 Fire" in California's Los Angeles County, the "Mosier Creek Fire" in central Oregon, and the "Pine Gulch", "Grizzly Creek" and "Cameron Peak" fires in Colorado.

August 15

More sharks were on the radar, this time in a New Jersey river, according to 1010 WINS. Authorities in Rumson warned residents about reported bull shark sightings in the Navesink River near Navesink Avenue in the borough.

August 16

"All we want is life beyond the Heat Dome," Tina Turner should have been singing as AccuWeather alerted that the western U.S. would be experiencing such containment with days of record high temperatures. "A heat wave for the record books is underway across the western United States, which is leading to complications with not only the drought and wildfire situation, but also the power grid in one state," AW stated. "The intensity and duration of the heat is likely to put a strain on people visiting the many national parks and hiking trails across the region, as well as long-time residents who may be more accustomed to extreme conditions. This is especially true for those left without power and air conditioning due to rolling blackouts."

Due to the excessive heat driving up energy use, the California Independent System Operator (ISO) declared a statewide Stage 2 emergency. The ISO later declared a Stage 3 emergency and started initiating rotating power outages. "Extreme heat throughout the West has increased electricity usage, causing a strain on the power grid. All available resources are needed to meet the growing demand," ISO said in a statement. Power to a little over 50,000 customers was shut off in California, according to PowerOutage.us.

AW suggested that electricity demands would continue to be pushed to the max for several days to follow as temperatures reached levels 15-30 degrees Fahrenheit above late-summer averages. Excessive heat warnings and heat advisories stretched from California and Arizona, to Washington and Idaho.

At the same time, dry lightning, heavy wind gusts and rare thunderstorms were pummeling San Francisco, CA's Bay Area, sparking vegetation fires and causing numerous large power outages, said ABC News 7. According to Meteorologist Drew Tuma, the lightning strikes started in San Luis Obispo. Fellow Meteorologist Lisa Argen said there were 326 lightning strikes in 30 minutes around the 6 a.m. hour.

Bay Area fire crews were working to put out several brush fires after the storms moved through the area.

August 17

Speaking of remarkable lightning, a photographer captured an eerie and majestic "sky jellyfish" image during a storm back in early July in western Texas, discovered Business Insider. "If you've ever looked up during a thunderstorm and glimpsed a red jellyfish sitting high in the sky, you weren't hallucinating. These tentacle-like spurts of red lightning are called sprites. They're ultrafast bursts of electricity that crackle through the upper regions of the atmosphere – between 37 and 50 miles up in the sky – and move towards space," said BI, citing the European Space Agency.

The phenomenon is rare: It lasts just tenths of a second and can be hard to see from the ground since it's generally obscured by storm clouds. But Stephen Hummel, a dark-skies specialist at the McDonald Observatory, captured a spectacular image of one of these sprites on July 2 from a ridge on Mount Locke in Texas.

"Sprites usually appear to the eye as very brief, dim, grey structures. You need to be looking for them to spot them, and oftentimes I am not certain I actually saw one until I check the camera footage to confirm," Hummel told BI.

You'd be better off dead than experience the blistering temp Death Valley reached, reported by CBS News. The thermometer at Death Valley's Furnace Creek, located in the deserts of Southern California, soared to 130 degrees Fahrenheit, according to NOAA's Weather Prediction Center. It was the hottest temperature recorded in the U.S. since 1913, and perhaps the hottest temperature ever reliably recorded in the world. The historic reading was just a small part of the massive, intense and long-lasting Heat Dome smothering the West Coast, that was only expected to get worse.

Before the heat record, the highest temperature ever recorded on Earth was *also* observed in Death Valley — 134 degrees Fahrenheit (in 1913). However, many experts contend that that temperature reading, along with various other temperatures recorded that summer, was likely an observer error. The hottest temperature ever "reliably" recorded previously on Earth was 129.2 degrees, in 2013, again in Death Valley.

August 18

The 2020 hurricane season continued to twist and take on a life of its own. USA Today shared that forecasters had heightened the odds of two systems becoming tropical storms or depressions in the Atlantic, as Hurricane Genevieve roared in the Pacific.

In the Atlantic, one system, in the eastern Caribbean Sea, had a 60% chance of development over the next five days. "A tropical depression could form late this week or this weekend when it reaches the northwestern Caribbean Sea," forecasters said. The second system was far out in the Atlantic, about halfway between Africa and the Caribbean, and was producing a concentrated area of showers and thunderstorms. Forecasters said a tropical depression was likely to form within the next day or two, putting the odds at 70%.

August 19

The Sacramento Bee wondered if California could handle so many wildfires at once. Already compromised by the COVID-19 pandemic, California's ability to fight its wildfires was being severely strained by a rash of lightning strikes and stupefying array of new fires. As major fires burned from Lake County to the South Bay, Cal Fire told TSB they were struggling to keep up with 367 new fires that had broken out over the past three days, the result of nearly 11,000 lightning strikes.

"Firefighting resources are depleted as new fires continue to ignite," said Jeremy Rahn, a Cal Fire spokesman, at a press briefing in Calistoga about the fires burning in the North Bay. He said Cal Fire had asked out-of-state agencies to rush 375 fire engines to the state and share "hand crews" and other resources. "The demand for hand crews far surpasses available resources," he said. All told, about 6,900 firefighters were deployed across the state, but the agency was seeking help from wherever it could.

Overhead, more Pop Rocks passed by Earth. LiveScience said that a compact car-sized asteroid made the closest Earth flyby a space rock has ever survived. Initially labeled ZTF0DxQ, and later formally dubbed 2020 QG, the rock swooped by Earth August 16 at a mere 1,830 miles away.

The flyby wasn't expected and took many by surprise. In fact, the Palomar Observatory didn't detect the zooming asteroid until about six hours after the object's closest approach. "The asteroid approached undetected from the direction of the sun," Paul Chodas, the director of NASA's Center for Near Earth Object Studies, said. "We didn't see it coming."

The close flyby was also a fast one: 27,600 mph.

August 20

A tornado touched down in New Jersey knocking out power for hundreds of people, said WCBS 880 News Radio. The National Weather Service confirmed the touchdown, in Lincroft, which left a path of downed trees and power outages weeks after Tropical Storm Isaias wreaked havoc in the same area. Officials said the small EF0 tornado, which packed estimated winds of 80 mph, first struck a baseball field at Brookdale Community College in the Lincroft section of Middletown. The weather service said the twister was able to send a set of metal bleachers flying and moved through a residential area, tearing up trees.

August 21

NPR gave a heads-up that two hurricanes could form in the Gulf of Mexico next week, an apparent first. At present, the tropical systems,

Marco and Laura, were heading toward that area and both were expected to become hurricanes before they neared the U.S. mainland early next week, according to the National Hurricane Center. Forecasters predicted both storms would hit near Louisiana — Marco first, then Laura. "If that were to occur, it would be the first time on record that the Gulf of Mexico has had two hurricanes at the same time," Meteorologist Philip Klotzbach said via Twitter. Louisiana had recorded multiple hurricane landfalls in one calendar year only four times since 1851, with the shortest recorded time in between landfalls recorded at around 17 days in 1860.

Out west, San Francisco Bay Area fires had joined the Top Five in California history, with regard to scope and damage, said the Los Angeles Times. The fires had killed at least five people, destroyed 629 structures and scorched more than 1,400 square miles.

Some seventy miles south, in the Santa Cruz region, wildfires continued to burn an area larger than the state of Rhode Island — more than 918,000 acres of forest and shrub lands.

August 23

Tropical Storm Marco became Hurricane Marco and moved into the Gulf. Behind it, Tropical Storm Laura was nearing the Florida Keys, said the South Florida Sun Sentinel. Based on an updated forecast track, each storm was expected to make landfall at hurricane strength in Louisiana, west of New Orleans, with Marco landing first, and Laura about 60 hours later.

In advance of Marco and Laura, Texas Gov. Greg Abbott declared a state of disaster in 23 counties and requested assistance from the federal government, said The Texas Tribune.

August 24

There was a bright spark (and not the flammable kind) amidst devastating fires in the Boulder Creek, California, area: 2,000-year-old redwoods survived wildfires in Cali's oldest state park, the renowned Big Basin Redwoods State Park, said NBC News. "When a massive wildfire swept through, it was feared many trees in a grove of old-growth redwoods, among the tallest living things on Earth, may finally have succumbed. But an Associated Press reporter and photographer hiked in and confirmed most of the ancient redwoods had withstood the blaze. Among the survivors is one dubbed Mother of the Forest," NBC related.

Hurricane Marco lost strength as it crossed the Gulf and ultimately made landfall near the mouth of the Mississippi River as a weak tropical storm, NPR reported. Regional attention had shifted focus to Tropical Storm Laura, which had "Louisiana and Texas residents bracing for what could be the strongest storm since 2005's Hurricane Rita — still ranked as the most intense tropical cyclone on record in the Gulf of Mexico."

August 25

The San Francisco Chronicle showed a heartbreaking photo of 72-year-old Ken Albers wiping his head as he took a break from sifting through the charred remains of his destroyed vintage Chevys, 16 in all, which were all melted and blackened — destroyed like the rest of his Vacaville home, from the LNU wildfires, north of San Francisco.

Down south, storm alerts were ramped up a notch, said ABC News. In Southeast Texas, residents in Galveston and Port Arthur were ordered to evacuate as Tropical Storm Laura strengthened in the Gulf of Mexico to hurricane strength en route to its expected landfall. The storm was forecast to make landfall as a major Category 3 hurricane with winds of up to 115 mph.

August 26

Here in southwestern Connecticut, News Channel 3 offered some advance warnings for tomorrow, calling for rain, hail, wind and even a possible tornado touchdown — all remnants of Storm Marco that was moving northeast since making landfall in the Gulf of Mexico.

August 27

Hurricane Laura roared ashore on the border of Texas and Louisiana as a Category 4 storm, ripping apart buildings, severing power lines and clogging streets with debris as a dangerous storm surge trailed behind, reported USA Today. Power was knocked out to over 800,000 customers and four deaths were reported in Louisiana. "With sustained winds of 150 mph, Laura's eye made landfall near Cameron, Louisiana, at about 1 a.m. CDT before plowing a path of destruction north toward Arkansas, where the weakened storm was predicted to then curve east through Kentucky and Tennessee," USA Today detailed. By noon CDT, sustained winds had dropped to 50 mph, and Laura became a tropical storm, forecasters said. Although the storm had weakened, forecasters continued to warn of flooding danger.

August 28

Connecticut Fish and Wildlife wondered: "Have you misplaced your Gar?" after finding a dead one washed up along the banks of the Farmington River in Farmington, in the central part of the state. The fish is not native to Connecticut and did not belong there at all. Gars are currently found in the United States from the Great Lakes basin in the north, and south through the Mississippi River drainage to Texas, Mexico and Florida.

The CFW had found other fish over the years that were out of place, including Pacus, Oscars, Goldfish and Plecos, as well as more familiar fish like Pike, White Perch, Alewife and other bait species.

CFW suspected the Gar had been illegally released into the environment, without a liberation permit. It explained that the permitting system was in place to protect local fish communities from introduction of potentially invasive species, disruption of the ecosystem and damage to existing fisheries, and to prevent introduction of diseases.

Coincidentally, a Connecticut woman happened to hook a "monster" pike, tying a 40-year-old record, according to FOX News. Leslie Slater was fishing by kayak with her family in Colebrook's West Branch Reservoir when she reeled in the impressive catch, the CT Department of Energy and Environmental Protection reported. All was calm until she felt a "huge hit", Slater said. "It pulled hard right to the bottom. It almost broke my pole in half," the angler said. "Then with all of the dead weight, I thought that I had lost the fish and snagged the bottom." Slater managed to pull the catch into her boat, later revealed to be a 29-pound, 46-inch Northern Pike. "Never in my life did I expect to see a freshwater fish of that size come out of Connecticut. The adrenaline rush pulling in a fish that size was awesome," she continued. "I still can't believe I pulled it into my kayak without flipping over or having my toes bitten off."

Certainly not a fishy tale, though also Connecticut-based: a severe thunderstorm that originated in upstate New York and barreled southeast through Fairfield and New Haven Counties yesterday afternoon knocked out power to 13,675 customers in United Illuminating's service area. Particularly hard hit towns were North Branford, North Haven and Hamden, said the electric utility.

Our state's lights-out situation was absolutely nothing though compared to the pounding Hurricane Laura inflicted on Louisiana and Texas, said NPR, which included the initial report of 10 deaths and up to $12 billion in estimated damage. Five of those people died from carbon monoxide poisoning — at least one case involving the use of a generator without proper ventilation. Four people died from trees falling on homes, according to Gov. John Bel Edwards. And a man drowned after the boat he was on sank, a local radio station reported.

And yet, while Laura showed a staggering amount of power, its damage tally wasn't likely to come close to other strong storms such as Hurricanes Katrina and Harvey — the two costliest storms in U.S. history. Katrina caused an estimated $160 billion worth of damage in 2005; Harvey caused $125 billion in damage in 2017. A key reason was that, while Laura came ashore with 150 mph winds — crashing large trees into houses, ripping roofs off buildings and tossing vehicles around — it avoided densely populated areas such as Houston and New Orleans. Laura also did not stall or hover, which can sharply increase rainfall totals in a given area. It also failed to send a catastrophic storm surge inland (forecasters had warned of a surge up to 20 feet). If not for those factors, officials and analysts said, things could have been far worse. "Nine to 12 feet of storm surge is still a lot of storm surge," Edwards said as state officials took stock of the damage.

According to Forbes.com, Laura was the strongest storm that Louisiana, specifically, had experienced in 150 years. Forbes noted that its damage included the destruction of the Lake Charles weather radar, likely due to 160 mph wind speeds it recorded just prior to its demise.

And Laura wasn't done, said FOX News. Downgraded to a Tropical Depression after it made its aggressive landfall in the Gulf, it was moving through the Mid-Mississippi Valley and Tennessee Valley and expected to swoosh into the Ohio Valley. Remnants were then to move toward the Mid-Atlantic region, carrying heavy rain, strong winds and the risk of isolated severe storms all along its path.

Meanwhile, forecasters were already eyeing two more developing systems in the Atlantic, according to USA Today. The National Hurricane Center had identified one system in the central Atlantic; the other in the eastern Atlantic. Both, they said, had a 30% chance of development within the following few days. The Center said that, should the systems develop into named storms (attaining sustained winds of at least 39 mph), they would be tagged Nana and Omar.

Nowhere across the globe seemed safe. BBC News reported that a lightning strike killed 10 children playing football in Africa, in the northwestern Uganda city of Arua, after sheltering in a hut during a storm. Nine children, aged 13 to 15, were killed on the spot while another died on the way to a local hospital. Three survivors were sent to a regional hospital for treatment. The region had been experiencing severe rains coupled with thunder and lightning for some time. This was the worst accident of its kind in Uganda since 2011 when 18 children were killed at a school in the mid-western region. That year, 28 people also died from lightning strikes in a single week. Back in February 2020, four rare mountain gorillas were killed after being hit by lightning.

Karachi, Pakistan, was no better off. BBC News said the southwestern coastal city was experiencing heavy flooding resulting from "the worst rainfall since records began 89 years ago". The annual monsoon rain was particularly bad and the area reported to be "largely underwater, with roads turned to rivers, houses destroyed and people relocated to shelters."

August 29

Shocker. The National Weather Service announced, in its capital-letter way, for us here in Connecticut, with regard to a recent band of severe weather that pushed through, that: BASED ON A NATIONAL WEATHER SERVICE DAMAGE SURVEY DONE WITH THE CT DIVISION OF EMERGENCY MANAGEMENT & HOMELAND SECURITY AND LOCAL CT TOWN EMERGENCY MANAGEMENTS, IT HAS BEEN DETERMINED THAT A STRONG EF1 TORNADO, WITH MAXIMUM WIND SPEED OF 110 MPH, TRACKED SOUTHEAST FROM BETHANY TO NORTH HAVEN CT, ON THURSDAY AFTERNOON, AUG. 27."

The NWS continued, "THE TORNADO FIRST TOUCHED DOWN IN A FORESTED AREA TO THE SOUTHEAST OF JUDD HILL RD IN BETHANY CT. THE TORNADO TRACKED SOUTHEAST OVER PRIMARILY FORESTED AREAS FROM AMITY RD. TO MUNSON RD. TOWARDS LITCHFIELD TPKE, CREATING A PATH OF DAMAGE ABOUT 75 YARDS WIDE, WITH HARDWOOD TREE DAMAGE CONSISTENT WITH WIND SPEEDS OF 80 TO 90 MPH.

THE PATH OF DAMAGE WIDENED TO AROUND 300 YARDS AS THE TORNADO TRACKED SOUTHEAST TOWARDS LAKE BETHANY. STRUCTURAL DAMAGE, INCLUDING SIGNIFICANT ROOF DAMAGE TO SEVERAL HOMES, AND SNAPPED HARDWOOD TREES, INDICATED WIND SPEEDS OF AROUND 100 MPH IN THIS AREA."

More: "THE TORNADO PATH CONTINUED SOUTHEAST FOR ANOTHER 4 MILES TO NEAR THE TOWN CENTER OF HAMDEN, CT, WITH TREE AND STRUCTURAL DAMAGE INDICATIVE OF WIND SPEEDS OF 70 TO 80 MPH. THE INTENSITY PICKED UP SIGNIFICANTLY AS THE TORNADO APPROACHED THE CENTER OF HAMDEN, AS EVIDENCED BY EXTENSIVE DAMAGE TO NUMEROUS BUILDINGS, INCLUDING THE FLAT ROOF OF A 2-STORY BUILDING ACROSS FROM HAMDEN TOWN HALL BEING TORN APART. WIND SPEEDS WERE ESTIMATED TO BE AROUND 100 MPH BASED ON THE DAMAGE TO THESE

BUILDINGS, BENT METAL FENCING AROUND TOWN HALL, AND UPROOTED AND SNAPPED TREES."

The wrap-up: "THE TORNADO REACHED MAXIMUM STRENGTH AND WIDTH FROM THIS POINT ON AS IT CONTINUED SOUTHEAST ACROSS WILBUR CROSS PARKWAY, I-91, AND DOWN TO THE INTERSECTION OF ARROWDALE AND THOMPSON ST. IN NORTH HAVEN, CT. TREMENDOUS HARDWOOD TREE DAMAGE AND STRUCTURAL DAMAGE WAS INDICATIVE OF WIND SPEEDS OF 110 MPH AND AN EXPANDED WIDTH OF 500 YARDS. IT WAS AT THIS POINT THAT THE TORNADO DISSIPATED WITH ITS DESTRUCTIVE STRAIGHT LINE WINDS FANNING OUT TO THE COAST."

So there was that. Our second occurrence of confirmed tornadoes here in the state in 2020.

August 31

We here in Connecticut hoped for calmer times as summer started to bid farewell and fall started to inch in. On this last day of August, local weatherman Paul Piorek reminded us that the Full Corn Moon was to debut September 2, at 1:22 a.m. EDT.

Wild Temps, Giant Craters & Space Rocks

September 1

And along with Moon announcements, we here in the Northeast got an official Fall Foliage forecast, suggesting colors would come sooner and last longer as a result of mostly dry conditions over the summer, according to the state Department of Energy and Environmental Protection, as reported by NBC CT. "Current conditions are setting the stage for an earlier start to the fall foliage season, with 'peak color' happening not all at once, but lasting several weeks in parts of the state," Connecticut State Forester Chris Martin stated. "Only a few regions of the world have seasonal displays of color like New England. And Connecticut offers some of the most diverse tree species in the region, which means a wider array of colors — yellow, bronze, orange, red and purple — for all to enjoy longer." Along with that prediction though, NBC Connecticut Chief Meteorologist Ryan Hanrahan said it may not be the most *colorful* season. "Lots of brown leaves from severely drought-stressed trees... plus almost fully bare trees down by the Sound due to Isaias and sea spray. Not exactly a recipe for good colors!"

Meanwhile, down in the Caribbean, one of the storms the National Hurricane Center had been tracking, did in fact develop into a Tropical Storm, Nana, stepping up south of Jamaica to become the earliest N storm in the already record-setting hurricane season, said FOX News. The storm system was about 110 miles south of Negril, Jamaica, moving west at 18 mph and packing maximum sustained winds of 50 mph.

Way overhead, more rocks were shooting past our turbulent planet.

Space.com raised an alert about an asteroid the size of a jumbo jet and its anticipated close encounter with Earth today, zooming past at about one-third the average distance to the Moon.

Named Asteroid 2011 ES4, it was expected to make its closest approach just after Noon EDT, according to NASA. At that time, it would be about 75,400 miles from Earth. Because the object's orbit wasn't well known, it had the potential of passing even closer than that, at a distance of just 45,400 miles, NASA added.

"Will Asteroid 2011 ES4 hit Earth? No!" NASA's Asteroid Watch outreach arm chirped on Twitter. "2011 ES4's close approach is 'close' on an astronomical scale but poses no danger of actually hitting Earth." The big rock measured somewhere between 72 feet to 161 feet in diameter. During its close approach, it was calculated to be traveling at a speed of 18,253 mph.

September 2

Looking back on the summer, The National Weather Service assessed that it was the hottest on record for *dozens* of U.S. cities, not just those aforementioned in this #because2020 narrative. Destinations like Phoenix, Tucson and Sacramento hit high marks, related ABC News. Phoenix, the country's sixth-largest city, saw average temperatures of about 96.7 degrees — almost 1.6 degrees above the previous summer record, the NWS said. Meanwhile, cities like Palm Springs, CA; Las Vegas, NV; Vero Beach, FL; Flagstaff, AZ; and Sarasota, FL saw their hottest *August* temperatures ever.

Other cities, including Bridgeport, CT; Hartford, CT; and Miami, FL tied their previous summer temperature records. ABC News offered a list "so far" of the cities across the country that had their hottest summer on record:

Phoenix, AZ: 96.7

Naples, FL: 84.6

Caribou, ME: 66.9

Harrisburg, PA: 77.9

Tucson, AZ: 90.0

Burlington, VT: 72.3

Portland, ME: 70.5

NYC - LaGuardia, NY: 79.5

Providence, RI: 74.4

Charlottesville, VA: 78.8

Norfolk, VA: 81.3

Cape Hatteras, NC: 81.7

Manchester, NH: 74.4

Bradford, PA: 67

Dubois, PA: 70.3

Burlington, VT: 72.3

State College, PA: 73.5

Tampa, FL: 84.8

Sarasota, FL: 84.6

Brainerd, MN: 71.1

As we wiped our brows reading this account, CNN checked in to announce that South and North Korea were bracing for two typhoons this week. The storms threatened to bring more flooding and devastation to an area that had already been battered by one of the wettest monsoon seasons in recent history.

Typhoon Maysak, the equivalent of a Category 4 hurricane, was expected to make landfall on the southern part of the Korean Peninsula. The storm was packing winds of 130 miles per hour but was expected to weaken to a Category 2 storm with winds of around 99 to 108 mph by the time it made landfall on the Korean Peninsula. If it made that landing, it would be the fourth named storm to achieve that this year. The Korea Meteorological Administration (KMA) expected South Korea to be hit by heavy rains and strong winds.

Its partner in weather crime, Tropical Storm Haishen, was expected to strengthen into a typhoon within 24 hours before becoming the equivalent of a Category 4 hurricane by the end of the week. It was expected to threaten Japan's southwestern Kyushu region first, and then potentially affect the Korean Peninsula. Japan's meteorological agency warned that the storm could be the third biggest to hit the country since records began almost 70 years ago.

September 3

Weather news didn't seem to get any better with the gradual transition from summer to fall. NBC News announced "Over 20 million people in the mid-Atlantic face the threat of severe storms, while California braces for 'record-setting heat' expected to be even more intense than the heat wave that gripped the region in mid-August and contributed to massive, destructive wildfires. Another four million people are under flash flood watches in parts of the South and Midwest."

The National Oceanic and Atmospheric Administration specified, "From a hazards perspective, it is the Desert Southwest and throughout California's Great Valley that stand out most with record breaking high temps likely this weekend and into early next week. About 44 million people were under excessive heat watches and warnings across the Southwest and West Coast, with high temperatures expected to possibly reach from 104 to 117 degrees in cities like Phoenix and Las Vegas and up to 95 degrees in San Diego."

The National Weather Service added, "More than 100 daily record-high temperatures will likely be set, including several all-time record highs."

With regard to the 2020 Atlantic hurricane season, it was continuing to show no sign of slowing, observed AccuWeather. Tropical Depression 15 had developed off the coast of North Carolina and officially become Tropical Storm Omar, joining already evolved Tropical Storm Nana. Nana had then strengthened to a Category 1 hurricane with 75-mph winds and made landfall on the coast of Belize. Omar gradually fell apart well northeast of Bermuda until it finally dissipated. Forecasters said that while a couple of days of rest for the season would be likely, there were areas already being monitored for development in the central and eastern Atlantic Ocean.

September 4

A 13-year-old Massachusetts boy caught a rare blue lobster — a 1 in 200 million find — according to USA Today. UT related, "Adam Carpenter couldn't believe his eyes. As he opened the lobster trap, he could see one of the crustaceans was visibly different from the others. The 13-year-old kept rubbing his eyes to make sure it wasn't a mistake. Yep, one of the lobsters was definitely blue. 'I'd seen YouTube videos of blue lobsters before but never thought I would catch one,' said Adam, who just got his lobster license this summer. 'I was shocked.'" UT said blue lobsters were indeed a rarity – a color mutation that happens about once in 200 million, according to the University of Maine Lobster Institute.

Holy holes! MotherBoard related that a mysterious 164-foot deep crater had suddenly opened up in the Arctic tundra in Siberia, Russia. It was apparently nothing new, however. Craters like these had been found since 2014. Scientists believed they were a result of cryogenic eruptions — in other words, ice volcanoes. According to the Siberian Times, a TV crew from station Vesti Yamal observed the massive crater by chance while traveling from an assignment. The hole had joined several others dotting the Yamal and Taymyr peninsulas in Siberia.

These geological phenomena had been the subjects of research for years. One group, led by Lomosnosov Moscow State University geologist Andrey Bychkov, proposed that the first discovered crater in the region was caused by an ice volcano eruption. The geologist stated that cryovolcanism is a known phenomenon on other planets, but prior to their study, ice volcanoes were not believed to exist on Earth. However, he found that a cryogenic eruption would adequately explain how the crater was formed. Prior to Bychkov's suggestion, it was theorized that the craters had been caused by meteorite impacts or the deep migration of gas under the Earth's surface.

September 6

CNN forecast that record cold temperatures and a rare September snow would arrive this week in the Rocky Mountains, the result of a strong cold front set to drop out of Canada in the beginning of the week, making its presence known from the Dakotas all the way down to Texas. CNN said that would bring a dramatic temperature swing to a large portion of the country as others dealt with record-breaking, triple-digit heat over Labor Day weekend.

"Nowhere is this temperature roller coaster more pronounced than in

Denver, where a 60-degree drop in the city's high temperature, from 99 degrees to 37 degrees, is expected in a mere 48-hour period," CNN said. "Such a front will bring a rare measurable snow to the Rockies. In fact, the higher elevations of the Rocky Mountains could pick up more than eight inches of snow. This would be one of the earliest first measurable snowfalls on record for the area, which typically doesn't see the powder begin piling up until October."

Frost advisories and freeze warnings were also possible with temperatures settling some 40 degrees below normal in the Rockies, Plains, Midwest, and even parts of the South. Meanwhile, excessive heat was expected to continue to impact the East Coast and West Coast with little reprieve expected for at least a week.

September 7

A somber milestone had been reached in the western United States: California wildfires set a record with more than two million acres scorched, the San Francisco Chronicle shared. "Fire crews battled numerous blazes across the state as high temperatures and ominous winds meant thousands of people across California were facing expected power shut-offs. With the new fires roaring over the holiday weekend, flames have burned more than two million acres in California this year, setting a dismal record," the SFC detailed.

The fires forced evacuations and the closure of national forests throughout the state and prompted daring rescues, highlighting the extremes that the year's fire season had brought. The new blazes came even as firefighters gained a handle on the big fire complexes burning around the Bay Area, said SFC.

Cal Fire said 14,800 firefighters were battling 23 major fires in the state, the Associated Press reported. California had seen 900 wildfires since Aug. 15, many of them started by an intense series of thousands of lightning strikes. There had been eight fire deaths and more than 3,300 structures destroyed. The previous record for acres burned was set in 2018. Fires that year burned 1.98 million acres and killed more than 100, most of them in the deadly Camp Fire that raced through the Butte County town of Paradise, the SFC said.

Fires on one coast, hurricanes on the other seemed to be a dominant 2020 pattern. "Hurricane Names Are About To Run Out As 2 New Storms Form Within 6 Hours", Forbes anxiously proclaimed. "The 2020 Atlantic hurricane season is continuing to chug along at a record pace with Tropical Storm Paulette and Tropical Storm Rene forming over a period of just six hours Monday, as forecasters warn most of the strongest storms lie ahead."

This particular week was historically the peak of hurricane activity in the Atlantic basin, with the exact peak coming on Sept. 10. To this point in 2020, 17 named storms had formed, making the year's season already above average, and putting it on a pace unseen since record-keeping began in 1851.

There were only four storm names left on the season's list, and the National Hurricane Center was monitoring two more systems that could develop this week. The SFC said that, if more than 21 storms form, further names would be used based on letters in the Greek alphabet. As we had learned back in early August, that had only happened once before, in 2005, when there was a record-setting 28 named storms, including destructive hurricanes like Katrina, Rita and Wilma. Now this was looking more like a reality.

Tropical Storms Paulette and Rene were both expected to strengthen, with Rene forecast to become a hurricane, but they weren't expected to impact any large land masses over the next week as they moved across the central Atlantic.

September 8

"From 100 Degrees to Record Earliest Freeze", Weather.com sheeshed, confirming what forecasters days earlier had suggested would happen. "The Front Range of the Rockies has a reputation for major temperature changes in a short amount of time, but what happened [in the last few days] took it to a record-breaking level. Denver hit 101 degrees on Sept. 5, the latest in the year that the Mile High City has hit the century mark since records began. Just three days later, [today], Denver tied its record earliest first freeze, previously set on that day in 1962."

As it hit its earliest freeze, Denver also had its second-earliest measurable snow, shattering the city's previous record for the fewest number of days (38 days in 2019) between the final 100-degree day of the year and the first measurable snow.

September 9

Australia recorded its first fatal shark attack on its Gold Coast beaches in 60 years, according to BBC News. An Australian man, Nick Slater, 46, was killed in a shark attack at Greenmount Beach at Coolangatta — a well-known surf spot — when a shark mauled his leg. Nearby surfers found him floating in shallow water next to his board. He was rushed to shore and given first aid but died at the scene. The city's mayor, Tom Tate, confirmed it was the first shark death at a Gold Coast beach since 1958.

September 10

Hurricane-force winds in Utah flipped 45 semi-trucks, killed one person and knocked out power to thousands of people, reported FOX News. "Wind gusts of nearly 100 mph roared through Salt Lake City as a system that caused a snowstorm over the Rockies gave the state a 40-degree temperature drop," the news station said.

September 11

"Vicious little suckers" became the phrase of the day after USA Today reported: "Massive clouds of mosquitoes kill cows, horses in Louisiana after Hurricane Laura". The paper said that swarms of skeeters had killed cows, deer, horses and other livestock in the Pelican State after rain from Hurricane Laura led to an explosion in the pests' population. The insects drained their blood and drove the massive creatures to pace in summer heat until they were exhausted, according to a Louisiana State University AgCenter veterinarian.

While recent aerial spraying efforts had helped bring the outbreak of mosquitoes under control, residents and animals in a portion of the state faced clouds of the bloodsucking insects in the days after Laura made landfall as a Category 4 hurricane on Aug. 27. Farmers near where the storm made landfall had probably lost 300 to 400 cattle, said Dr. Craig Fontenot, a large-animal veterinarian based in Ville Platte.

Jeremy Hebert, a LSU AgCenter agent in Acadia Parish, told USA Today that residents along costal, marshy areas are accustomed to mosquitoes and expect the population to climb following a heavy rain. But the scale of this outbreak was much larger than Hebert expected: "I've never experienced anything like this."

September 12

Residents of our Connecticut shoreline were warned about an illness caused by bacteria in salty or brackish water, said NBC CT. The warning came from the state's Dept. of Public Health after an unusually high number of infections along Long Island Sound were recorded. Since July, five cases of Vibrio vulnificus infections had been reported to the DPH.

Experts said one patient was from Fairfield county, one patient was from Middlesex county and the other three were from New Haven county. All five were between the ages of 49 and 85 years old. Two of the patients had an infection of the bloodstream and three had serious wound infections, authorities said. All five patients were hospitalized and no deaths were reported, they added. Investigators said all five patients reported exposure to salty or brackish water during activities such as swimming, crabbing and boating.

The infection was described by health experts as extremely rare. In the past 10 years, between 2010 and 2019, only seven cases were reported in Connecticut, experts said. It can "cause wound infections when open wounds are exposed to warm salt or brackish water (mix of salt and fresh water). Once inside the body, the bacteria can infect the bloodstream, causing septicemia. Infected people can get seriously ill and need intensive care or limb amputation, the DPH said. About one in five people with this type of infection actually die — sometimes within a day or two of becoming ill. Those at the greatest risk for illness were those with weakened immune systems and the elderly," they added.

And Sally was her name-o. Tropical Storm Sally, that is, and she was headed for New Orleans, according to USA Today. Sally was "expected to strengthen into a hurricane, bringing with it the possibility of a life threatening storm surge for areas of the Gulf Coast. The National Hurricane Center issued a hurricane watch from Grand Isle, Louisiana, to the Alabama-Florida border — an area that included metropolitan New Orleans."

Sally was the earliest S-named storm on record in the Atlantic, said meteorologist Philip Klotzbach of Colorado State University, beating the previous record-holder, Stan, which formed in October 2005.

On the upside, Klotzbach said, "While we have had a tremendous number of named storms this year, we have only had one major hurricane so far this year (Laura). However, Paulette may become a major hurricane in the next few days."

September 13

A battle was on to save Brazil's tropical wetlands from flames, said NBC CT. A vast swath of the region was burning, with fire sweeping across several national parks and dense smoke obscuring the sun. "Preliminary figures from the Federal University of Rio de Janeiro, based on satellite images, indicate that nearly 5,800 square miles have burned in the Pantanal region since the start of August — an expanse comparable to the area consumed by the historic blazes now afflicting California. It's also well beyond the previous fire season record from 2005," NBC reported.

Brazil's National Institute for Space Research, whose satellites monitor the fires, said the number of Panantal blazes in the first 12 days of September was nearly triple the figure for the same period last year. From January through August, the number of fires more than tripled, too, topping 10,000.

September 14

Folks in Connecticut were "ticked off" to learn about the discovery of Asian longhorned ticks in the state. Eyewitness News 3 said The Connecticut Agricultural Experiment Station (CAES) had discovered the first established population of the insect in Connecticut. Scientifically known as Haemaphysalis longicornis, it was found in Fairfield County.

"The Asian longhorned tick is an invasive species that was initially discovered on a farm in New Jersey in 2017, raising public and veterinary health concerns, and has subsequently been found in at least 14 other states," the CAES stated. Experts said the tick is native to Japan, and parts of Russia and China. It's also a major livestock pest in Australia and New Zealand.

Dr. Goudarz Molaei, a research scientist directing the CAES Passive Tick Surveillance and Testing Program, said his team would be closely monitoring the tick and human biting activity, "as well as its potential involvement in transmission of exotic and local disease agents."

We wished ticks were our only troubles after learning from CNN that five tropical cyclones were confirmed to be currently present in the Atlantic at the same time — for only the second time in history. The only other time this had occurred was in 1971. The current five systems were Hurricane Paulette, Hurricane Sally, Tropical Storm Teddy, Tropical Storm Vicky and Tropical Depression Rene.

Sally's front edge was expected to reach the northern coast of the Gulf of Mexico later today and make landfall soon after, the National Weather Service warned. Hurricane warnings extended from Morgan City, Louisiana, to the Mississippi/Alabama border. Impacts from Sally of an extremely dangerous and life-threatening storm surge, hurricane-force winds and torrential rain with flash flooding were anticipated later today.

And quicker than you could slap a crawfish on a grill, Sally intensified into a Category 2 hurricane, The Weather Channel alerted, aimed at the Mississippi coast.

And while it was all hands on deck in the Gulf, Oregon was ablaze. CNN said, in particular, that wildfires scorching the West Coast had devastated the small city of Detroit, about 120 miles southeast of Portland, where a majority of the structures in the rural enclave had been flattened. "We have approximately 20-25 structures still standing, and the rest are gone," officials with the Idanha-Detroit Rural Fire Protection District noted on their Facebook page. City Hall, where the fire department's district office is based, was one of many buildings that had burned down.

"Our primary focus is protecting the structures that are still standing," the officials added. "Several of our firefighters have also lost their homes. They are working through their own losses while also fighting to protect homes still intact."

Resident Elizabeth Smith lost everything in the wildfires. "Our homes are absolutely destroyed. I've seen a few videos and photos and my lovely little house that we remodeled 12 years ago in this beautiful canyon area is absolutely flattened. It looks as though a bomb went off," she remarked.

Detroit Mayor Jim Trett compared his city's devastation with that of Paradise, California, which was destroyed in the Camp Fire in 2018. "It's the same topography: three canyons coming down like a funnel into the city of Paradise at the bottom of the funnel," Trett said.

September 15

Birds were dropping dead in New Mexico, potentially in the "hundreds of thousands", said NBC News. "It appears to be an unprecedented and very large number," Martha Desmond, a professor at New Mexico State University's department of fish, wildlife, and conservation ecology, said. State residents had reported coming upon dead birds on hiking trails and missile ranges, and in other locations.

Multiple agencies were investigating the occurrences, including the Bureau of Land Management and the White Sands Missile Range, a military testing area. "On the missile range, we might, in a week, find or get a report of less than half a dozen birds," Trish Butler, a biologist at the range, shared. "This last week we've had a couple hundred, so that really got our attention."

It was unclear to scientists why the die-off was occurring. Desmond said it was possible it was caused by a cold front that hit New Mexico last week or by recent droughts. She speculated it might also be related to the wildfires in the West. "There may have been some damage to these birds in their lungs. It may have pushed them out early when they weren't ready to migrate," she said.

And speaking of those western fires, California blazes had, to date, burned an area almost the size of Connecticut (over 3.2 million acres of land), according to Eyewitness News 3. CalFire added that nearly 16,500 firefighters had been battling 28 major wildfires in the state, which had left 24 people dead and over 4,200 structures destroyed. For those who had avoided the flames, smoke from the fires had choked the air and kept people inside. The continued risk of future fires had also forced partial power shutoffs for thousands of California residents. "These are intense, huge blazes," said billionaire environmentalist Tom Steyer. "This is a huge, immediate, urgent problem."

The fires on the West Coast were so massive, in fact, that smoke was drifting across the entire United States, said Rocky Hill, CT-based WFSB. "Here in Connecticut, you may have noticed the sky is hazy, due to this drifting smoke."

Birds dropping, fires blazing… and sea ice dramatically melting in the Arctic. EcoWatch said that Arctic sea ice had reached its annual minimum, bottoming out at its second-lowest extent and volume ever recorded, behind 2012. A new study suggested that the 2012 record hadn't yet been broken (despite ever-rising temperatures) because the rapidly-warming Arctic had altered the jet stream, leading to cloudy summer Arctic conditions that had acted to temporarily preserve some of the sea ice. However, long-term global warming would inevitably win out, said EcoWatch, and scientists expected the Arctic to be ice-free in the summer beginning sometime between 2030 and 2050. Overall, three-quarters of the volume of summer sea ice in the Arctic had melted over the past 40 years.

September 16

Sally made landfall as a Category 2 hurricane near Gulf Shores, Alabama, delivering catastrophic flooding and severe widespread damage, relayed FOX News, from the Baldwin County Emergency Management Agency in Alabama, which reported an "extremely dangerous situation."

In Florida's Panhandle, officials shut down Interstate 10 at Escambia Bay Bridge near Pensacola due to sustained high winds. Many other roads were also shut down due to flooding in that area. The regional NWS forecast office said major storm surge flooding was reported in downtown Pensacola, with at least three to four feet of water. Car alarms there were triggered, setting off honking horns and flashing lights that illuminated floodwaters up to the bumpers of parked cars. More than two feet of rain was recorded near the Naval Air Station in Pensacola. Sally also knocked out a section of the new Three Mile Bridge in Pensacola as the storm pounded the Gulf Coast with wind and rain.

At least 40 people had to be rescued, including a family of four found in a tree. Pensacola's sheriff said that thousands of people in the communities he served would need to be evacuated from rising water in the coming days.

Meanwhile, Michiganders were dealing with another sort of misery: confirmation of a case of the mosquito-borne Eastern equine encephalitis virus, according to USA Today, which Connecticut had encountered in early June. An adult in Barry County was suspected of having the virus. As a precautionary measure, 10 Michigan counties were urged to cancel outdoor events that take place at dusk. Also known as Triple E, the virus is one of the deadliest mosquito-borne diseases in the United States, with a 33% fatality rate in people who become ill. It leaves many survivors with physical and mental disabilities, and kills 90% of the horses sickened by the virus. Cases had been confirmed in 22 horses in the 10 Michigan counties that were urged to cancel outdoor events.

As Michiganders were running from skeeters, smoke from the U.S. West Coast wildfires had shot past the East Coast, drifted across the Atlantic Ocean and reached Europe, said CNN. The fires, which began in mid-August in California and Colorado, were "significantly more intense than the 2003-2019 average for the whole country and the affected states," according to data from Europe's Copernicus Atmosphere Monitoring Service (CAMS). Oregon and Washington had also seen serious wildfires break out since the beginning of September, following recent hot, dry and windy conditions.

Scientists from CAMS (part of the European Centre for Medium-Range Weather Forecasts) use satellite observations to track wildfire activity around the world. "The scale and magnitude of these fires are at a level much higher than in any of the 18 years that our monitoring data covers, since 2003," said Mark Parrington, a senior scientist for CAMS. "A good indicator of smoke thickness is aerosol optical depth (AOD). Over the western U.S., AOD levels have been observed to reach values of seven or above. To put this into perspective, an AOD measurement of one already implies very hazy conditions and potentially poor air quality."

Some calm amidst all the world chaos: critically endangered pink dolphins had returned to the waters around Hong Kong, due to Covid lockdowns, announced the New York Post. "It seems very quickly that the dolphins have come back into this waterway," marine researcher Lindsay Porter said of the miraculous resurgence. Indeed, sightings of the rare marine mammal — also known as the Chinese white dolphin and Indo-Pacific humpback dolphin — had shot up almost 30% since the region halted boat and ferry traffic in March over COVID concerns. In turn, this "very quiet" environment allowed researchers to monitor the species with drones and underwater microphones. "What we have noticed since the ferries have stopped in this area is dolphins we hadn't seen for four, five, six years are back in the Hong Kong habitat," said Porter, who had studied the animals for three decades in Hong Kong.

But let's refocus the narrative to zombies for a minute. Open Culture shared that the Pentagon had created a plan to defend the U.S. against a zombie apocalypse. "For keen observers of pop culture, the floodtide of zombie films and television series over the past several years has seemed like an especially ominous development. As social unrest spreads and increasing numbers of people are uprooted from their homes by war, climate catastrophe and, now, COVID-related eviction, one wonders how advisable it might have been to prime the public with so many scenarios in which heroes must fight off hordes of infectious disease carriers? Zombie movies seem intent, after all, on turning not only the dead but also other living humans into objects of terror," OC mused, setting the stage for its news. "The genre's history may go some way toward explaining why the U.S. government has an official zombie preparedness plan, called CONOP 8888."

The document was apparently written in April 2011 by junior military officers at the U.S. Strategic Command (USSTRATCOM) as a training exercise to formulate a non-specific invasion contingency plan. Despite the use of a "fictitious scenario," CONOP 8888 explicitly states that it "was not actually designed as a joke", according to OC.

An excerpt from the Plan begins, "Zombies are horribly dangerous to all human life and zombie infections have the potential to seriously undermine national security and economic activities that sustain our way of life. Therefore having a population that is not composed of zombies or at risk from their malign influence is vital to U.S. and Allied National Interests."

The Plan, said OC, as you might expect, details a martial law scenario, noting that "U.S. and international law regulate military operations only insofar as human and animal life are concerned. There are almost no restrictions on hostile actions… against pathogenic life forms, organic-robotic entities, or 'traditional' zombies.'" So there was that.

September 17

Hurricane Sally really did a number on Florida, CNN confirmed. "We had 30-plus inches of rain in Pensacola, which is four months of rain, in four hours," Ginny Cranor, chief of the Pensacola Fire Department, said. In Escambia County, which includes Pensacola, at least 377 people had been rescued from flooded neighborhoods, Jason Rogers, the county's public safety director, told reporters in a news briefing. "It's going to be a long time, folks … to come out of this thing," Escambia County Sheriff David Morgan added. A Gulf Shores, Alabama, beach area resident described the damage: "Looks like a war zone. Lots of destruction, homes destroyed, roofs gone. I have not had any service, power or internet. Bad night."

September 18

ANOTHER giant crater appeared on Siberia's Arctic tundra, said Newsweek. The latest depression — 650 feet wide — was found on the Gydan peninsula, a region to the east of the Yamal peninsula, where a 165-foot crater was found Sept. 8.

This *latest* crater was found by Oleg Shabalin, head of the nearby Gyda village. He reported the find, thinking it may have formed through an explosive release of methane as others like this were known to develop, which was becoming "increasingly common throughout the tundra zone of Russia," he said. However, scientists said this depression, which was "only" 65 feet deep and filled with sludge, likely formed as a result of warm temperatures, with ice trapped in the permafrost melting and causing the soil to collapse. Marina Leibman, from the Earth Cryosphere Institute, part of the Russian Academy of Sciences, confirmed that the formation was a "thermocirque".

As the U.S. was being battered by hurricanes, Greece was getting blasted by Storm Ianos, a rare "medicane" — an unusually powerful storm system in the Mediterranean, according to Insider. It had recorded high winds in excess of 70 mph and was expected to dump large amounts of rain. The phenomenon happens less than once a year. A report by the BBC showed images of boats being battered in a harbor on Kefalonia and damage to a sidewalk and fencing on Zakynthos.

As a rule, medicanes were less powerful than Atlantic hurricanes. According to CNN, Ianos was roughly equivalent to a strong tropical storm in the Atlantic. Medicanes are usually more feared for their rains than their wind speeds, as well. CNN forecast that Ianos could drop nearly 10 inches of rain in some areas, with highs of nearly 20 inches in extreme cases.

September 19

That's just bats. No, really. The National Weather Service spotted a massive *bat* colony on its weather radar, according to CNN. "Murder hornets, zombie cicadas, invasive lizards — the list of icky pests popping up across the United States appears to be growing this year. Next on the list? Massive bat colonies, just in time for Halloween," CNN poked.

Apparently, meteorologists at the National Weather Service (NWS) in Phoenix were looking at their radar screens and spotted a large cloud of motion sweeping over areas of the city last week. "That doesn't look like a normal shower, the way everything is sort of fanning out," NWS meteorologist Sean Benedict observed at the time. "They don't really have a uniform direction. That's usually your clue initially that it's probably animals flying around."

His team quickly surmised that they were looking at an enormous colony of bats. They were spotted around sunset, suggesting that the critters were Mexican free-tailed bats that migrated to the city for the summer, Arizona Game and Fish Department biologist Angie McIntire ventured.

September 20

Hurricane Sally had another huge impact on the region as it pushed its way north: the deposit of thousands of starfish on Florida's Navarre Beach, according to USA Today. Danny Fureigh, chief of Navarre Beach Fire Rescue, said he had seen such a phenomenon only once before, a few years ago, but never anything of this magnitude. "There are thousands and thousands of them," he said, noting that they were present pretty much from the Turner House (the lifeguard headquarters) all the way to Opal Beach.

Fureigh suspected the mass starfish beaching had something to do with water toxicity following the hurricane. The water quality was so bad in Sally's wake that Navarre lifeguards flew double red flags. "You have this big surge of water coming inland from several miles out, and then washing back out with everything it touches," he said. "It's like a big toilet bowl, pretty much. We were the only beach flying double red flags because of the water quality. We wouldn't want our families swimming in that."

September 21

The mercury plummeted and records were shattered all over the Northeast, confirmed the U.S. National Weather Service's Eastern Region HQ. The most dramatic record-smashers included Houlton, ME: 23 (25 in 1950); Massena, NY: 27 (30 in 1962); Morrisville, VT: 27 (33 in 2010); Plattsburg, NY: 28 (31 in 1956); Saint Johnsbury, VT: 28 (34 in 2010); Saranac Lake, NY: 21 (25 in 1962); and Springfield, VT: 27 (34 in 2010).

EarthSky, in the meantime, alerted that a small, recently discovered asteroid — labeled 2020 SW — would be passing our planet a lot closer than the Moon's distance this week; even closer than our TV or weather satellites. "This approach is so close, and the asteroid is so small, that Earth's gravity will bend the space rock's trajectory," said ES, but "It will not hit us."

At its closest approach, EarthSky said the asteroid should pass at an estimated distance of 17,556 miles from Earth — just 0.0735 lunar distances. For comparison, television and meteorological satellites orbit at some 22,300 miles from our planet's surface.

September 22

In other space news, our astronauts housed in the International Space Station had to take shelter as their home away from home dodged orbital junk, said Space.com. Controllers maneuvered the station away from a potential collision with a piece of debris today by firing the thrusters on a Russian Progress cargo spacecraft that was docked to the orbiting lab's Zvezda service module, NASA officials said.

The three astronauts that were then aboard the station — NASA's Chris Cassidy and cosmonauts Anatoli Ivanishin and Ivan Vagner — sheltered in the station's Russian segment during the maneuver to be closer to the Russians' Soyuz spacecraft. That was done "out of an abundance of caution," NASA said. "At no time was the crew in any danger."

September 23

October was going to kick off with a mixed bag of weather across the U.S., said AccuWeather. They forecasted a massive shift in the weather pattern, with summer-like heat building over the West and a surge of Arctic air plunging into the eastern half of the nation. AW anticipated that both high and low temperature records could be broken amid the extreme weather setup. It added that frosts and freezes could threaten sensitive agriculture from as far south as parts of the Ozarks in northern Arkansas to the Blue Ridge Mountains straddling Tennessee, North Carolina and far northern Georgia.

The Pentagon had a zombie defense plan we learned, but did it ever anticipate a zombie *storm*? That's what FOX News was calling Hurricane Paulette, after it went out to sea to die, but instead regenerated as a "zombie" tropical storm. "In an Atlantic hurricane season that has broken records, a tropical system managed to come back to life a week after hitting Bermuda," reported FOX News, confirmed by the U.S. National Hurricane Center (NHC) in Miami.

Paulette had formed earlier in September and made landfall as a hurricane in Bermuda, with the island ending up directly in the eye of the storm. The storm had since weakened but had become a post-tropical cyclone for the second time, according to the NHC.

"Because 2020, we now have Zombie Tropical Storms," the National Weather Service (NWS) said on Twitter. "Welcome back to the land of the living, Tropical Storm Paulette."

Tragically, there was no chance that 380 long-finned pilot whales that had stranded themselves in Australia were going to come back to life. The Guardian confirmed the stranding — the worst in Australia's history and, likely, globally — in western Tasmania. More than 450 of the beasts were initially caught on sandbanks and beaches inside Macquarie Harbour. Seventy whales were rescued and coaxed back to the open ocean.

September 24

In other news out of Australia, dozens of giant robber crabs crashed an outdoor barbecue and swarmed a group of families, according to the Daily Mail. The families, at a campsite on Christmas Island, were cooking when crabby crustaceans showed up to their festivities looking for something to eat. One of the family members said that she had never seen so many of the creatures at one time before. "My son counted 52 of them," she said. "They started to climb up to the table, and another climbed onto the barbecue. We kept our tents away from where we had eaten, but one of the families said the whole night they could feel one tapping on the outside of their tent."

And while crabs were bombarding the barbie, a massive pack of hungry raccoons had staked out a San Francisco, CA, park, reported the New York Post. The group of 14 raccoons emerged from the bushes at Golden Gate Park, startling a father and son who snapped a picture of the bizarre scene. "It was so surreal…a posse of bandits…like out of a movie," the dad, Marc Estoque, said. "And then two minutes later there was a coyote. I was waiting for the unicorn to pop out."

The seemingly massive population of raccoons in the Bay Area had long been chronicled. As far back as 2008, there were reports of a "troubling raccoon inundation". The pack had grown over time as people fed them snacks, against park advisories.

September 25

Other pests — emerald ash borers — were threatening the future of North American Ash Trees, said Smithsonian. For 18 years, the trees had been under attack by the half-inch long, metallic green beetles. It had been a slow-moving battle, and scientists were just now beginning to understand the nationwide effects the beetles had on forest populations.

A study published in Forest Ecology and Management reported that the forests that had faced the initial beetle invasion had recovered the most new growth, but it was likely not enough to replace all of the trees that were lost. And that fact could lead to a downward trend and the eventual loss of North American ash trees altogether, a Science magazine reporter speculated.

Comparatively, over a century ago, the eastern United States was covered in nearly four billion American Chestnut trees. Now, the species is considered functionally extinct due to a deadly blight fungus introduced around the turn of the 20th century.

September 26

GEOMAGNETIC STORM WARNING! Westport (CT) Astronomical Society alerted that a solar wind stream was heading for Earth, and that it could spark the strongest geomagnetic storm in more than a year. NOAA forecasters said storm levels could reach category G2 (moderately strong) when the gaseous material arrived on Sept. 29. Bright "equinox auroras" were already dancing around the Arctic Circle. The WAS said that, if the G2-storm unfolded as predicted, Northern Lights could descend into upper-tier states as well.

As turbulent as the heavens, conditions over Alaska were agitated. The National Weather Service office in Anchorage issued a rare Hurricane Force Wind Warning for the state's Northern Gulf. The NWS said parts of the Gulf could experience waves as high as a three-story building as a result of the gusts. The warning extended up to 100 nautical miles out, including Kodiak Island and Cook Inlet.

And given these turbulent conditions up high and down low, it seemed little surprise that the Alps would get socked by an early snowfall. ABC

News said that parts of Switzerland, Austria and Germany had received an unseasonably early snowfall overnight after a sharp drop in temperatures and heavy precipitation. The Swiss meteorological agency said that the town of Montana, in the southern canton (state) of Valais, experienced nearly 10 inches of snowfall — a new record for this time of year. In parts of Austria, snowfall was recorded as low as 1,805 feet above sea level. Authorities were out in force across mountainous regions in the affected Alpine nations to clear roads blocked by snow and ice.

September 27

Move over Wright Brothers. Live Science trumpeted news of the Longest Non-Stop Bird Flight ever recorded. On Sept. 16, a male bar-tailed godwit (*Limosa lapponica*), known as "4BBRW", set off from southwest Alaska and flew for 11 days straight to New Zealand, traveling a distance of about 7,581 miles, taking rounding errors into consideration. The previous record was held by a female bar-tailed godwit that flew around 7,145 miles over nine days in 2007. Bar-tailed godwits are known to be impressive flyers, but 4BBRW's journey — prolonged by easterly winds — was extra impressive.

Mad cows? That seemed to be apparent with FOX News' report that a herd had charged and killed a man in England — the second in a month. The "tragic death" of 72-year-old Malcolm Flynn, of Carlisle, happened on Sept. 11 when he was walking near Thirlwall Castle and Gisland, Northumberland, according to police there. Flynn was with a companion when the cows charged across the field. He was pronounced dead at the scene — the Pennine Way, a national trail that stretches into Scotland. Over a week before Flynn's death, teacher Dave Clark died after cows injured him while he was walking near Richmond, North Yorkshire.

September 28

When a vacation wonderland goes bad… OX News said a tornado had touched down on South Carolina's Myrtle Beach oceanfront, sending beach chairs flying. The twister touched down near 74th Avenue North, according to the Myrtle Beach Fire Dept. Forecasters from the National Weather Service (NWS) confirmed the twister was an EF-0 tornado, with winds of 75 mph at the beach. While the area was not under a tornado warning at the time, the remnants of Tropical Storm Beta were moving through the area.

September 29

Just north, a woman found a rare two-headed snake inside her North Carolina home, said Newsweek. Jeannie Wilson, of Taylorsville in Alexander County, shared a video of the rare reptile on her Facebook profile, asking friends and family if the snake should be set free into the wild or donated to someone who could help care for it in captivity. Due to its appearance, Wilson nicknamed the snake "Double Trouble", which she believed to be a baby rat snake.

Based on the video, the snake's heads appeared to be working independently of each other and a flickering tongue could be seen emerging from each one. While difficult to determine from the clip alone, the left head seemed significantly more dominant.

The jet stream, meanwhile, had really wound itself up, ready to bring fire-provoking weather to the West and a chill to the East. National Geographic said the "supremely wavy, loopy" current was responsible for hot, dry weather that had returned to the western half of North America, and for a shock of cold headed for the middle and eastern parts of the U.S.

"The weather pattern across the United States is about to get wild," wrote Meteorologist Guy Walton. In his more than 30 years of weather forecasting, he said he had never seen such an extreme pattern set up at this time of year. His predictions had started to become reality. "We're looking at a whole week of record heat in the West," he anticipated, along with a "great blue trough" of cold air coming down from the Great Lakes to the Southeast.

The heat meant another round of dangerous fire weather for California and much of the West, which had already smashed past previous records for burning; more than 5.8 million acres had now gone up in flames to date. In contrast, in the East, folks were expected to feel weather that aligned more with the calendar.

Like Hurricane Sally had deposited thousands of starfish along the east coast the third week of September, Hurricane Teddy had now pushed seashells ashore along North Carolina's Outer Banks, according to Travel + Leisure. The beaches of the barrier islands were reportedly blanketed in seashells thanks to a perfect combination of storm winds, massive waves and lunar tides. Cape Lookout National Seashore shared a photo on Facebook showing a sprawling shell patch featuring sea treasures of all shapes, colors, and sizes left by Teddy. One commenter shared that her daughter had found more than 30 full-size conch shells, all intact, over the weekend. While Hurricane Teddy never made landfall in the U.S., its tropical-storm force winds generated massive waves compounded by the seasonal arrival of "King Tides."

Unfortunately, big storms have a way of moving other stuff around, too. The HuffPost reported that five miles of Florida beach had been slimed with oil, as a result of Hurricane Sally. Samples of the oil found on Perdido Key's Johnson Beach were collected in an attempt to determine the source of the pollution, according to the U.S. Coast Guard. It was possible the storm whipped up still-submerged oil from the 2010 Deepwater Horizon oil spill in the Gulf of Mexico or pushed the oil from another source onto the shore.

March of the Penguins? IFL Science said that Antartica's snowmelt had uncovered a hidden colony of mummified Adélie penguins. A study published in the journal Geology detailed the surprising discovery of the aquatic birds, preserved in remarkable condition thanks to the region's climate. Some of the remains were in such good shape that they appeared fresh. Lead researcher Steven Emslie said it was a confounding finding given that there were no records of an extant penguin colony at Cape Irizar since the first explorers came to the Ross Sea in 1901-1903.

Among the remains was a glut of penguin chick bones, which were scattered among guano stains left by the droppings of penguins at some point in the Cape's history, said IFL. Emslie and his team even came across some complete chick carcasses still with feathers falling away and other complete mummies. Perplexed by the inconsistencies of their findings with the Cape's record, they collected samples for radiocarbon dating to try and make sense of what they were looking at.

The analyses revealed that Cape Irizar had played host to breeding penguins on at least three occasions, with the last one ending around 800 years ago. It was possible this occupation came to an end as a result of increasing snowfall as it was at around this time the Little Ice Age was kicking in. The "fresh" remains found by Emslie's team were likely buried in snow when they died and preserved intact until recent snowmelt revealed them once more on the surface, IFL related.

Snowmelt had been occurring across the region as global warming pushed up the annual temperature of the Ross Sea by around 34.7 to 35.6F since the 1980s. The effects had been observed via satellite imagery, showing more and more of the cape emerging from beneath its icy cover.

"Overall, our sampling recovered a mixture of old and, what appeared to be, recent penguin remains, implying multiple periods of occupation and abandonment of this cape over thousands of years," stated Emslie. "In all the years I have been doing this research in Antarctica, I've never seen a sight quite like this. This recent snowmelt, revealing long-preserved remains that were frozen and buried until now, is the best explanation for the jumble of penguin remains of different ages that we found there."

Sadly, Down Under, Australia began disposing of over 350 dead long-finned pilot whales after ending its rescue mission of the massive beasts that had beached themselves a week ago on a remote sandbank in Tasmania's Macquarie Harbour, said CBS News. Of the 470 whales initially stranded, conservation experts and trained volunteers were ultimately able to save 108. Marine Conservation Program wildlife biologist Dr. Kris Carlyon stated that rescuers did a terrific job saving the whales, given the overwhelming event.

The cause of the stranding remained unknown. However, some researchers suggested the whales may have gone off track after feeding close to the shoreline or by following one or two whales that strayed.

September 30

DW shared that the world was on the brink of an extinction crisis and the window of opportunity was closing. "Stopping mass species extinction is possible if the world pulls together," said leading ecologist Gerardo Ceballos. Almost 40% of plants were at risk of extinction, scientists warned, and land clearing, over-harvesting of wild species and changing weather patterns all posed significant threats. Of the almost 4,000 new species of plant and fungi that botanists registered in 2019, many were already facing extinction. Researchers said they were now in a "race against time" to catalogue unknown species before they disappeared for good.

Ceballos is the founder of the Stop Extinction campaign, which aims to raise awareness about species loss. He co-authored a seminal 2015 paper defining what had become known as the sixth mass extinction. He suggests, "In the past, there has been what we call five mass extinctions. Those mass extinctions are basically of a catastrophic nature. They have caused the destruction of around 70% of all the animals and plants on the planet. And we call them mass extinctions because they're much, much higher than the normal background extinction. We found that species of vertebrates, mammals, birds, reptiles and amphibians that have become extinct in the last 100 years would have taken 10,000 years to become extinct under normal background extinction rates. In other words, in 100 years, we have lost species that would normally have taken 10,000 years to lose. In one year, we lost the species we would have lost in 100 years. That's the magnitude of the problem. So we conclude that we have entered the sixth mass extinction. And in this case, the sixth mass extinction is caused by humans."

Ceballos proffers that human population, consumption and the use of technologies like fossil fuels are the extinction causes. "Things that are more easily tracked, and that we can change, are habitat destruction and illegal trade — this gigantic enterprise run by international mafias in Mexico, the US, Europe, China that make a gigantic profit by exploiting species. This, plus things like air pollution, invasive species and, now, global warming is causing this mass die-off of populations and species. And what is very important to emphasize is that this sixth mass extinction is accelerating. Unless we do something, the rate of extinction will double," he said.

For the moment, it seemed like fishing boats off the coast of Spain were *more* endangered, with reports of killer whales ramming them, Newsweek shared. Reports of orcas attacking boats emerged at the start of September, though encounters started as early as July. One Spanish naval yacht lost part of its rudder after several orcas attacked it.

In an interview with the BBC, Scottish yacht owner Graeme Walker, whose vessel was attacked for 45 minutes early on September 22, described his encounter with three orcas: "The boat would literally spin 90 degrees when the animals came in. It was as pronounced as that. When they actually bit on the rudder and started shaking the rudder, the wheel was spinning from side to side. You could not have touched it. You would have broken your arms."

That same day, Spain's Ministry of Transport, Mobility and Urban Agenda banned sailing vessels that were 49 feet or less in length from sailing between Cabo Prioriño Grande and Punta de Estaca de Bares, where the killer whale attacks had taken place. This was done as a preventative measure to protect people on board and the killer whales.

"Interactions with killer whales have affected, above all, medium-sized sailboats," the ministry stated. "All the encounters with the killer whales took place between two and eight nautical miles from the coast and the sailing speed ranged between five and nine knots, either exclusively under sail, or sail and motor."

Justin Crowther, a British sailor whose yacht was attacked and had to be rescued, said that, after docking, he realized how close the orcas had come to overturning the boat. "I have sailed in Australia, Tahiti, Canada... all over the world... and I had seen orcas... but none had ever gotten this close."

Experts said that while this increase in killer whales attacking boats seemed extreme, the encounters were still relatively rare: only 20 percent of orca sightings from yachts had reported damage or trouble.

Having assessed footage of some of the attacks, researchers said they were carried out by two or three young animals. They noticed two of the killer whales were seriously injured, which may have prompted their behavior.

Alfredo López, a biology professor opined, "It's not revenge. They're just acting out as a precautionary measure. Our interpretation is that they don't have the slightest intention of attacking people."

October 2

Good grief, more Murder Hornets had been found in Washington state, said the New York Post. Officials there were on a search-find-and-destroy mission of a suspected Murder Hornet nest after more and more of the invasive insects were seen in the state's northeastern region, near the small town of Blaine. "We believe we are dealing with a nest," said Sven-Erik Spichiger, an entomologist. "We hope to locate it in a couple of weeks and eradicate it."

The Asian giant hornets were first seen in the state in early May. Agriculturalists worried that, if established, the hornets could threaten local honeybees that farmers in the region depend on to pollinate a wide variety of crops.

October 4

The California fire season set a staggering new milestone, with more than four million acres burned to date, the Los Angeles Times said, more than double the state's previous record. Over 8,200 structures had been destroyed and tens of thousands of people displaced.

Meanwhile, the 2020 hurricane season kept on chugging, as Tropical Storm Delta formed in the Caribbean, AccuWeather said. "While Tropical Storm Gamma continues to meander on the northern coast of the Yucatan Peninsula, a tropical depression in the central Caribbean Sea strengthened to Tropical Storm Delta and is forecast to strengthen and take aim at the central Gulf coast of the United States," AW shared.

A tropical low moving through the Caribbean Sea was first designated Potential Tropical Cyclone 26 by the National Hurricane Center. That became Tropical Depression 26 just south of Jamaica, with maximum sustained winds of 35 mph. The depression was then upgraded to Tropical Storm Delta and expected to rapidly intensify once pulled northward into the central Gulf of Mexico. It was currently about 270 miles southeast of Grand Cayman, moving to the west-northwest at around 9 mph. A tropical storm warning was issued for the Cayman Islands and a hurricane watch by the Cuban government for the Isle of Youth and Cuban provinces of Pinar del Rio and Artemisa. A tropical storm watch was also issued for the Cuban province of La Habana.

An ecological catastrophe? That's what investigators were trying to determine in Russia's Kamchatka region, according to NBC News, after scores of dead sea creatures washed up in one of its bays and surfers reported burns to their eyes and throats. Images of dead seals, octopi, starfish and urchins on the Khalaktyrsky Beach in the Avacha Bay were shared on social media for several days. Surfers in the area had also complained that the sea had an unnatural smell and color. Local government in the region, which is known for its pristine beaches and volcanic black sand, shared video of one surfer who said a number of wave riders like himself had suffered chemical burns to their eyes. He added that he had not seen anything like it in 15 years.

October 5

A Super-Pig uprising? Popular Mechanics said that might be the end result due to America's rapidly growing feral hog problem. "With nine million wild pigs and counting, the swine bomb is coming, experts warn. Are we ready?" PM asked.

The growing population included hybrid "super-pigs". Those and the robust fertility of agricultural pigs comprised the overall pack which, over 30 years, had expanded from 17 states to 39.

The 2017 film "Okja" posited a *Cujo*-like super-pig, but researchers said that idea is now close to a reality for some groups of feral pigs. That was because most wild pigs in the U.S. were some level of hybrid between domestic pigs and wild boars, creating heterosis or hyrbid vigor and a generation of wild pigs that can have the protective fur of the wild boar and the carefully bred huge litter size of the domestic pig, for example.

Pigs here, Tasmanian devils over there. CNN said the TDs were returning to Australia's mainland after 3,000 years. Eleven Tasmanian devils, in fact, had been released into a 988-acre wildlife sanctuary north of Sydney, New South Wales.

The devils died out on the mainland several millennia ago after the arrival of dingoes and were restricted to the island of Tasmania. Their numbers suffered another blow from a contagious form of cancer known as Devil Facial Tumor Disease (DFTD), which killed around 90% of the population since it was discovered in 1996. There were now just 25,000 wild devils left in Tasmania. A team released the 11 devils on September 10, following an earlier trial involving 15 of the marsupials, which meant 26 Tasmanian devils were now living in mainland Australia.

October 6

Yet more rocks hurtling past Earth, said the New York Post. "Tomorrow is a big day for close-approach asteroids as three are set to skim past Earth," the NYP shared. "The largest could be up to 272 feet wide — that's almost as big as the Statue of Liberty. All of the asteroids are on NASA's close approach list. The first pass will happen around 9:12 a.m. EST. That's when Asteroid 2020 RK2 is expected to come within a distance of 2.3 million miles of our planet."

NASA estimated that RK2 would be traveling around 15,000 miles per hour. And even though it would be millions of miles away, in the grand scheme of space, that wasn't a large distance at all. For that reason, NASA said it would be keeping an eye on the asteroid, along with the two that come after it on Oct. 7.

"Any fast-moving space object that comes within around 4.65 million miles is considered 'potentially hazardous' by cautious space organizations," the NYP noted.

After RK2, Asteroid 2020 TB was to be next, at 2:25 p.m. Estimated to be 223 feet wide, TB was expected to shoot past at 17,000 miles per hour around 2.7 million miles away from Earth.

Lastly, Asteroid 2019 SB6, measuring up to 85 feet wide and traveling over 17,000 mph, was expected to zoom by at 7:23 p.m. SB6 was to come closest to Earth of the three — around 2.1 million miles away at its closest point.

Thankfully, NASA didn't expect any of the asteroids to veer off course and impact Earth.

Meanwhile, a single wildfire in California had reached the stunning size of more than one million acres, becoming the first "gigafire" in the state in decades, according to VOX. The August Complex Fire in the northern part of the state had burned at least 1,003,300 acres and was just 54 percent contained, according to the California Department of Forestry and Fire Protection (Cal Fire). The area that it had burned since the fire ignited on August 16 was larger than Rhode Island and spanned seven counties.

The blaze was just one of almost two dozen major wildfires that were still burning in the Golden State in what had already been an extraordinary year for the sweeping infernos.

Meanwhile, the outcry from surfers complaining of poisoning-like symptoms after exposure to the water in the Kamchatka area of Russia drove the region's acting Minister of Natural Resources and Ecology, Aleksei Kumarkov, to analyze samples. These revealed the presence of petroleum products at levels four times what they should be, a more-than-doubling of expected levels of the even more toxic compound phenol, and other substances. Regional prosecutors opened an investigation into alleged pollution in the Kamchatka waters, but it remained unclear what the *source* of the chemicals might be.

October 7

2020 was really bringing it on: "Indiana Police Detective Dies After Being Stung by Hornets Over 40 Times" headlined People. The detective died at Rush Memorial Hospital in Rushville after he was attacked while hunting with a friend. According to an official report, the 59-year-old was removing a tree stand in the woods near Brookville when they were besieged. After being stung all over his body, he began to have issues with shortness of breath and collapsed in the woods. His death was ruled accidental and deemed a result of a heart attack caused by an allergic reaction.

Look up! It's a bird. It's a plane. It's a Draconid? IFL Science alerted stargazers that the Draconid Meteor Shower was about to peak. A yearly event, the Draconids were expected to peak the evening of October 8. While considered a minor shower in the past, with around five meteors an hour, it had been one of the most active in recent years, reaching a spectacular 1,000 meteors per hour several times across the 20th century. The shower put on particularly good shows in 2005, 2011, and 2012, with up to 600 seen an hour.

IFL explained that the shower is caused by Earth crossing the path of debris left over from the periodic comet 21P/Giacobini-Zinner, which orbits the Sun every 6.6 years. The most intense showers happen after the comet has come close to Earth's orbit, so 2020 was not expected to be exceptional. The comet wouldn't be circling back to the inner Solar System until 2025.

October 8

Hairy, venomous caterpillar spotted in eastern Virginia, CNN shared. Considered to be one of the most venomous in the U.S., the puss caterpillar was sighted multiple times in "parks or near structures". The Virginia Department of Forestry warned residents to stay away from the critter because it has venomous spines across its thick, furry coat. "There are little hollow hairs in that fluffy, hairy material," Theresa Dellinger, a diagnostician at the Insect Identification Lab at Virginia Tech, told CNN. "It's not going to reach out and bite you, but if someone brushes up against that hair, it'll release toxins that you'll have a reaction to."

That reaction might include an itchy rash, vomiting, swollen glands and fever, according to the University of Michigan. It'll also put you in a world of pain. A Richmond, Virginia, resident described the feeling like a scorching-hot knife. A Florida mother said her teenage son began screaming when "stung" by one.

The caterpillar isn't commonly found in the state. Sightings are more likely farther south, in states like Texas, or in midwestern areas like Missouri, according to researchers. No one was entirely sure why there had been so many recent reports in Virginia.

"With changes in our climate, we're seeing some insects change their population," Dellinger told CNN. "But it's too soon to tell. Caterpillars, moths and butterflies all have cyclical periods. It's all about the right time, and the right conditions."

October 9

Other weird stuff was turning up, but this time in Florida. Newsweek reported an enormous Burmese python caught there was the largest ever found in the state. The Florida Fish and Wildlife Conservation Commission (FWC) said the snake measured 18.9 feet in length — a new record for the

Sunshine State. The previous largest Burmese python caught in Florida was slightly smaller, measuring 18.8 feet, captured in 2013.

The latest record-breaking snake was caught October 2 near the L-28 Tieback Canal, about 35 miles west of Miami, by snake hunters who work with the South Florida Water Management District (SFWMD) and FWC respectively.

Native to Southeast Asia, Burmese pythons are an invasive species in Florida, where they became established in the southern part of the state around 20 years ago. It is thought they gained a foothold after pythons being kept as exotic pets were released or escaped. Population estimates for the python in Florida vary wildly because they are hard to detect, but it is thought the number could be over 300,000.

Because they have no natural predators in the region, they have been able to reproduce rapidly. They can live to around 20 years, and sexually mature females are capable of laying up to 100 eggs per clutch, once per year.

The U.S Geological Survey said the pythons were "one of the most concerning invasive species" in the Everglades National Park because they compete with non-native wildlife for food, and eat native animals. Scientists have linked significant population declines in some mammal species, such as raccoons, opossums and bobcats, to the Burmese python invasion.

In an attempt to combat the spread of this invasive species, the state introduced a python elimination program in 2017, jointly managed by the FWC and SFWMD.

Wap. Wap. Wap. No that wasn't a python smacking its tail on the ground, but the sound of birds colliding one after another into Philadelphia skyscrapers. CNN reported that up to 1,500 of them may have flown into the buildings, *in a single day.* "Traumatic" was the only word Audubon Pennsylvania volunteer Stephen Maciejewski could find to describe the event. Typically, he patrols a certain downtown area every morning to count and collect dead birds or identify injured ones that need to be rescued. But on the morning of Sunday, October 2, he quickly realized there were far more birds than he was used to retrieving. Hundreds more. "I've never seen anything like this," Maciejewski said. "There were birds everywhere, and they were all dead." Maciejewski had begun collecting the fallen birds at 5:30 a.m. Two hours later, he realized he needed backup. He called Keith Russell, the program manager for urban conservation for Audubon Pennsylvania. Maciejewski, Russell and other volunteers were able to collect 400 birds, most of which were dead, others injured. But they weren't able to reach every building they needed to that day. Thus, they estimated the birds they found represented just one-third of the deaths -- meaning the total could be anywhere between 1,000 and 1,500.

Audubon Pennsylvania suspected that the mass deaths in Center City started the previous night. Peak migration season, which typically begins in the fall, combined with poor weather conditions, may have led to the incident, it said. "Philadelphia is along the Atlantic Flyway, so the birds are migrating through the city in gigantic numbers," Russell told CNN. "With lots of clouds and rain, and the bright lights that come from buildings, they get disoriented and gravitate towards towers or buildings that are nearby." Some of the species found that day included warblers, thrushes, vireos and sparrows.

October 12

Meteor or space junk? That's what NASA was pondering about a newly discovered asteroid, said CBS News. Instead of a cosmic rock, the newly discovered object appeared to be an old rocket from a failed moon-landing mission 54 years ago that was finally making its way back home, according to NASA's leading asteroid expert. Continued observation was expected to confirm its identity.

"I'm pretty jazzed about this," said Paul Chodas, manager of the Center for Near-Earth Object Studies (CNEOS) at the Jet Propulsion Laboratory (JPL) in California. "It's been a hobby of mine to find one of these and draw such a link, and I've been doing it for decades now."

Chodas speculated that Asteroid 2020 SO, as it was formally known, was actually the Centaur upper rocket stage which, before it was discarded, successfully propelled NASA's Surveyor 2 lander to the moon in 1966.

The lander ended up crashing into the moon after one of its thrusters failed to ignite on the way there. The rocket, meanwhile, swept past the moon and into orbit around the sun as intended junk, never to be seen again — until perhaps now.

October 14

A fisherman caught a two-headed baby shark off India's Maharashtra coast, potentially the first of its kind in that region, according to HuffPost. The fisherman tossed it back into the water, but not before taking photos of the rare find. Biologists checked out the images of the six-inch fish and determined it was either a spadenose or sharpnose shark.

Two-headed mutations had become more common, but no one knew exactly why. National Geographic offered a few possible factors for the malformations, including pollution and a "dwindling gene pool due to overfishing." Still, this latest discovery was unusual.

October 16

More fishy things were going on in coastal Massachusetts. Emergency officials in the Wareham area received numerous calls about a creature in Broad Cove, said FOX News. Apparently, people thought it was an injured seal, a shark or a stranded fish. It turned out to be a giant ocean sunfish. Also called mola, sunfish are the heaviest bony fish, with the largest weighing almost 5,000 pounds, according to National Geographic. Sunfish are "clumsy swimmers," according to the magazine, and often come near the surface to enjoy the sun. However, they have a huge dorsal fin that can get them mistaken for a shark -- which is what happened in Wareham. After police received call after call about the sunfish, the Wareham Department of Natural Resources posted on Facebook asking residents to *stop* reporting it.

October 19

A British supermarket sent a single chicken nugget to space, said Travel + Leisure. It was unclear if the nugget underwent special training before its mission, T+L mused.

"Lots of things have been sent up into space: Cookie dough. $23 million dollar toilets. But this might be the first time fast food has boldly gone where no fast food has gone before. According to The Irish News,

British supermarket chain Iceland Foods Ltd. launched a chicken nugget into space on Oct. 13 in order to celebrate the store's 50th anniversary," T+L relayed.

"2020 is a huge year for us as we celebrate our birthday, and we wanted to find ways to mark the occasion, just like anyone celebrating a birthday in lockdown," said Andrew Staniland, Iceland Foods' trading director. "What better way to show that our products are out of this world then by sending one of our customer favorites into space."

Iceland Foods teamed up with space marketing company Sent Into Space in order to organize the launch, according to CNN. The nugget was taken to a launch site in rural Wales, where it was sent via a gas-filled weather balloon to Near Space, about 20.7 miles up, traveling at about 200 mph to get there, The Irish News reported. The UK outlet calculated that this was a distance of about 880,000 chicken nuggets. Near Space is the area between Earth's atmosphere and outer space. It begins at 12 miles above sea level, while Outer Space begins around 62 miles, said CNN.

The nugget floated in Near Space's low pressure atmosphere for about an hour before descending back to earth via parachute. Since it was a frozen nugget, it seemed to be indifferent to the incredibly low temperatures of space, according to the Sent To Space website. It was safe to say that the breaded food had become a hero to chicken nuggets everywhere.

October 22

A Colorado woman's pet deer gored a neighbor, then, with bloody antlers, threatened a wildlife agent, said NBC News. The deer, which a Colorado woman raised from fawn to buck, had to be euthanized, according to state officials.

The deer's owner, Tynette Housley, 73, of Black Forest — about 20 miles northeast of Colorado Springs — was issued two misdemeanor citations connected to the illegal keeping of wild animals, according to the Colorado Department of Parks and Wildlife (CPW).

From a hospital bed, the unnamed victim told the department that she was "surprised to notice the deer following her, and then shocked when it attacked, knocking her down and thrashing her with its antlers." The deer continued to attack until she squeezed between two cars in her garage, the department said. "The victim suffered serious lacerations to her head, cheek and legs ... and was hospitalized overnight for treatment of her injuries before being released," NBC noted.

October 24

No, it was not a Moon landing, but a Murder Hornet Operation, the Daily Beast noted, as entomologists garbed in bulky protective white suits from head to toe tracked the pervasive, invasive insects to a tree in Washington state. A tweet from the Washington State Department of Agriculture said it all: "Got 'em."

In gear designed to keep the insects' long stingers away from their skin and venom out of their eyes, they descended before dawn on a tree in Blaine. The whole scene looked like a cross between a lunar touchdown and a low-budget sci-fi flick as the team suctioned away the first Murder Hornet nest found in the United States.

A few days earlier, entomologists had managed to trap several of the Asian giant hornets and affix tiny radio tracking devices to them with dental floss, if you can imagine that. One of the trio led the insect hunters right to the nest. While the fearsome bugs usually nest in the ground, dozens and dozens had made their home inside the cavity of a tree on property that had been cleared for a new home.

The goal was to capture as many of bugs as possible. So, under the cover of darkness, with red lamps their only light, the moon-suited crew wrapped the trunk in plastic. Then the ambushed hornets were carefully vacuumed out of the tree and into a plastic cylinder that state officials proudly showed off on social media.

October 26

Water was discovered on the sunlit part of the moon for the first time, NASA said, as reported by USA Today. The revelation indicated water may be distributed across the *whole* lunar surface, and not just limited to its cold, shadowed places, such as the poles. This was good news for astronauts living in future lunar bases who would be able to tap into those resources for drinking and rocket fuel production.

Paul Hertz, director of the astrophysics division in the science mission directorate at NASA headquarters in Washington, said "This discovery challenges our understanding of the lunar surface and raises intriguing questions about resources relevant for deep space exploration."

October 27

NASA was *also* psyched about Psyche, "16 Psyche" that is, one of the most intriguing and most valuable asteroids we know of, said Forbes. About 230 million miles from Earth, Psyche is one of the most massive objects in the Solar System's main asteroid belt orbiting between Mars and Jupiter. It's about 140 miles wide and — unlike most asteroids, which are rocky or icy — appears to be metallic. In fact, it's so dense and metallic that Psyche is thought to be the leftover core of a planet that failed during its formation — a "protoplanet." It may have been struck by another object and lost its mantle and crust.

"We've seen meteorites that are mostly metal, but Psyche could be unique in that it might be an asteroid that is totally made of iron and nickel," said Dr. Tracy Becker, a planetary scientist at the Southwest Research Institute in in San Antonio, Texas, and author of a related paper published in the *Planetary Science Journal*. Iron and nickel are often found in metallic meteorites and in the dense metal cores of planets. Earth, for instance, has a metal core, mantle and crust.

Psyche is truly a one-of-a-kind object in the Solar System, and some think that the metals that comprise the asteroid may be worth about $10,000 *quadrillion*. For comparison's sake, our entire global economy was worth about $142 trillion as of 2019.

October 28

A dog gave birth to a puppy with fur that was a bright, garish shade of green, the Independent shared. The unusual phenomenon occurred in North Carolina, when a white German Shepherd named Gypsy gave birth to a litter of eight puppies. Everything about the birth occurred as one would have expected, apart from when the fourth puppy made his arrival. "The puppy's green hue is likely to have been caused by meconium, a puppy's first feces, which may have been passed ahead of birth, or placental pigments," Daniella Dos Santos, president of the British Veterinary Association, suggested.

Further south, in southeastern Louisiana and Mississippi, the latest Atlantic storm terror, Hurricane Zeta, with a Category 2 intensity, had made its way into the Gulf and come ashore with high winds, heavy rain and a life-threatening storm surge, according to the National Hurricane Center, as reported by CNN. Racing along at 25 mph, Zeta made landfall with winds of 110 mph.

October 29

The National Hurricane Center (NHC) announced the formation of Tropical Storm Eta, according to AccuWeather. With Zeta hardly in the rearview mirror and officials and residents still assessing damage along the Gulf Coast and across the Southeast, forecasters had shifted their attention to the newest threat. Nearly one month was still left in the season, set to officially end on Nov. 30. Eta was the 28th named tropical storm of the season, tying 2005's record of 28 named systems in one year. This was also the first time the name Eta had ever been used in the Atlantic basin.

The NHC had been ratcheting through the Greek alphabet — for only the second time in history — to name tropical systems once the designated list for 2020 was exhausted. 2005 was the only other year to use Greek letters, and Zeta was last on the list for that notorious season. Eta was birthed as Tropical Depression 29, forming 315 miles southeast of Kingston, Jamaica, with maximum sustained winds of 35 mph. The depression strengthened to Tropical Storm Eta with maximum sustained winds of 40 mph. Eta was cruising along at 15 mph to the west.

October 30

NBC Connecticut reported the state's first snowfall of the season — only the fifth time Connecticut had seen snow during the month of October since 1905. Northern CT's higher elevations were expected to see two to four inches of snow altogether.

Thump…. thump…. thump. "Earth Keeps Pulsating Every 26 Seconds. No One Knows Why." headlined Popular Mechanics. Indeed, our planet had been having a "microseism" every half minute, possibly forever. In the early 1960s, a geologist named Jack Oliver first documented the pulse. While working at Columbia University's Lamont-Doherty Geological Observatory, Oliver heard the noise but didn't have at his disposal the advanced instruments seismologists have now. Since then, scientists have spent a lot of time listening to the pulse and even finding out where it comes from: a part of the Gulf of Guinea called the Bight of Bonny. Some researchers think the pulse has a kind of prosaic cause. Under the world's oceans, the continental shelf acts as a gigantic wave break. It's the boundary off the very far edge of, for example, the North American continental mass where the highest part of the plate finally falls off into the deep abyssal plain. Scientists have theorized that, as waves hit this specific place on the continental shelf in the Gulf of Guinea, this regular pulse is produced. If that sounds improbable, consider all the different shapes of drums, from timpani to bass drums to bongos, that you hit with your hands. It's not impossible that just one shape of continental shelf "drum" would create the right harmonic bang to rattle the Earth. If that's true, we're probably lucky it's *just* one.

October 31

A full moon on Halloween? Sure, climb aboard the 2020 Crazy Train. WTNH said that, for the first time since the 1940s, Halloween would be extra spooky due to a full moon this year. For many, the pairing would be a once-in-a-lifetime event. The last time it occurred was in 1944, according to the Farmer's Almanac, and the next one wasn't expected until 2039, according to NASA. The moon would also be a "blue" one, though it wouldn't actually appear to be blue. Scientists use the term to describe the second full moon of a given month, which only occurs about once every 2.5 years, NASA said.

According to the Farmers Almanac, the first full moon of 2020 howled onto the scene with January's Wolf Moon on Jan. 10. And usually, we have one full moon for each month, making the total 12 for the year. But on occasion, some months will have two full moons, like this month. There was a full moon on Oct. 1 — the Harvest Moon — which usually appears in September.

November 1

We here in Connecticut were expecting some gustiness, and not from the consumption of chili bubbling in pots on stovetops this time of year, but from high winds expected throughout the southern portion of the state that would bring a cold front pushing overnight lows into the 30s, the Darien Times alerted.

Rain would also spill forth, accompanying the 10-15 mph winds, according to the National Weather Service, which had issued a small craft advisory for Long Island Sound and other offshore areas. The first push was going to be followed by gales on the Sound, New York Harbor, Peconic and Gardiners Bays, and South Shore bays from Jones Inlet through Shinnecock Bay. Wind gusts up to 46 miles per hour were expected, pushing seas up three to five feet. "Strong winds will cause hazardous seas which could capsize or damage vessels," warned the NWS, advising boaters to stay in port, secure vessels or seek safe harbor.

Our windy, choppy conditions were nothing though, compared with what was happening in the Philippines, according to EcoWatch. Super Typhoon Goni, dubbed "the strongest landfalling tropical cyclone in world recorded history", had absolutely clobbered Bato, Catanduanes Island, Philippines and the surrounding region, with sustained winds of 195 mph and a central pressure of 884 mb as it came on shore, according to the Joint Typhoon Warning Center (JTWC). Early reports shared that the beastly storm had killed 31 people, damaged or destroyed 250,000 homes, and caused over $1 billion in estimated damage, tying it with Typhoon Bopha in 2012 and Typhoon Vamco in 2020 as the Philippines' second-most expensive typhoon on record, adjusted for inflation. Only Super Typhoon

Haiyan in 2013 ($11.1 billion) was more damaging. Ominously, seven of the 10 strongest landfalls in recorded history had occurred since 2006, according to EcoWatch.

November 3

Boy, that was a long stretch. In an alarming illustration of Arctic sea ice melt, EcoWatch shared that the Northern Sea Route along the northern coast of Russia *finally* froze shut today, after being open a record 112 days. On the upside (for the gas industry, anyhow), it resulted in 2020 being the busiest *shipping* season ever for natural gas tankers in the Arctic, according to Bloomberg.

November 4

Astronomers discovered a "hellscape" planet that rains rocks, has lava seas and clocks winds of more than 3,000 mph, reported the New York Post. Dubbed K2-141b, the planet exists more than 200 light years away and is one of the "most extreme" ever discovered, according to a just-published paper in the Monthly Notices of the Royal Astronomical Society.

Scientists said K2 is flanked by winds four times the speed of sound and has an ocean of lava more than 60 miles deep. The planet also has temperatures that plunge on one side to negative 328 degrees Fahrenheit — so frigid that it can freeze nitrogen. On the other side of the planet, temperatures rise to 5,432 degrees Fahrenheit, which is scorching enough to vaporize rock. Scientists said the extreme heat allows the rocks to precipitate as if they were particles of water.

Similar to Earth, the particles follow cycles in which they evaporate, rise into the atmosphere, condense and then come back as rain. But on K2-141b, the evaporated particles are pulled to the frigid side by supersonic winds — causing rocks to rain back down into the lava ocean, the NYP shared.

November 6

Virginia had another nightmarish creature pop up on its landscape. FOX News reported that a creepy, snake-sized invasive worm had been spotted — and it's "essentially immortal". A foot in length, the invasive species slithered by a suburban Virginia resident last week, leaving pest-control experts scratching their heads before they found help identifying it.

In a since-removed Facebook post, local pest control service Virginia Wildlife Management and Control wrote that its hotline had received a call about a weird looking "snake" in Midlothian, Va., just outside Richmond. "The problem is, we've never seen anything like it before, and we're not sure if it's a freak of nature," the company wrote. It turned out that it wasn't a snake at all but an invasive hammerhead worm, according to a follow-up post.

Hammerhead worms are native to Asia and feed on normal earthworms and other organisms in the soil -- and sometimes cannibalize themselves. And, like common earthworms, when cut in half, both sides remain alive and continue to grow, rendering them hard to kill — or essentially immortal, as one commenter put it.

November 8

An earthquake off the coast of Massachusetts. 2020 was really putting on a show. The quake was felt all across New England, said FOX News. The U.S. Geological Survey (USGS) confirmed the temblor as a magnitude 3.6, centered a few miles off the coast of New Bedford, Mass., in Buzzards Bay. No damage or injuries were reported but it sure shook up the region.

November 10

Storms swept through the Chicago area as a cold front ended a record-breaking week of 70-degree temps, according to the Chicago Sun-Times. The strong winds and thunderstorms even triggered a tornado watch for much of northern Illinois and southern Wisconsin, according to the National Weather Service. A wind gust of 79 mph was recorded at Aurora

Municipal Airport in the west suburb. Chicago's police urged motorists to watch out for downed trees and power lines on roads; the CTA reported train service delays due to debris on the tracks as the storms moved in from the west over the city. The severe weather lasted about an hour or two in any spot, the weather service said.

The severe weather ended seven straight days of 70-degree November weather, blowing past the previous five-straight days of similar weather in 1953. In a complete flip-around, real-feel temps were anticipated to plummet into the 20s in the storm's wake.

November 11

In a disturbing situation follow-up report, FOX News said that, among 500 Murder Hornets that had been found and destroyed late last month in that nest in Blaine, Washington, were nearly 200 queens capable of starting their *own* nests.

"It really seems like we got there just in the nick of time as our original vacuum extraction seemed to only give us workers," said Entomologist Sven-Erik Spichiger, with the Washington State Dept. of Agriculture. "We only got queens four days later after we cracked it open, and so if any queens had already left the nest, it was just a few."

A horrific mass tragedy, in the meantime, was taking place in Denmark, BBC News reported. The country made the decision to cull all its mink — up to 17 million animals — after authorities worried that a mutated form of coronavirus found in the animals could potentially hamper the effectiveness of a future vaccine. The cull was directed by the prime minister, who deployed police and the armed forces across the countryside and to farms, to cull all the animals. Mass graves, filled with the slaughtered animals, had already begun to appear across the country.

The task was expected to take a long while. "We have 65,000 mink," said Farmer Martin From, who pointed to rows of long huts that housed his herd of mink in rural Funen. "In the coming week, all will be put down." Overnight, he had seen his livelihood wiped out. He flew a Danish flag at half-mast in his garden. "It seems very unjust," he added.

The national cull had begun to evolve into a political outcry after the prime minister admitted the plan was rushed and had no legal basis.

November 13

The Weather Channel issued an alert that Tropical Depression 31 had been designated, forecast to become record-breaking Hurricane Iota. And, unfortunately, it had its sights set on Central America, which had just been devastated by Eta. The latest storm was expected to be packing 110-mph winds as it made landfall on the east coast of Nicaragua.

November 16

A prehistoric fish with a long snout and five rows of bony plates on its back washed ashore on Virginia Beach's oceanfront, said the Virginia-Pilot. People walking on the beach near 20th Street stopped to take pictures of the Atlantic sturgeon as the tide slowly dragged the decomposing carcass back into the water. Sturgeon are an endangered species. In the fall, females lay eggs in the rivers of the Chesapeake Bay, and then migrate offshore, said Noelle Mathies, a marine biologist, who specializes in sturgeon research. The sighting was eyebrow raising because of the fish's strange appearance, but also because of its size: five feet in length.

Sturgeons have existed for more than 120 million years and were around when dinosaurs roamed the earth. They can live up to 60 years, said the VP. Their mouth works like a vacuum, sucking up clams and other mollusks, crustaceans, worms and insects, according to the Chesapeake Bay Program, a restoration group.

November 17

Whooooosh. What was that? Oh, just a low-orbit asteroid zipping by Earth. BGR said a small asteroid made an extremely close flyby of Earth recently and wasn't detected until after it had already passed. Known as 2020 VT4, it flew past at a distance of just *240 miles*. It was closer to Earth during its flyby than many man-made satellites and even the International Space Station.

"Our solar system is packed with rocks. We're living on one of them right now, in fact, but most of the rocks in our little stellar neighborhood are much smaller," BGR noted. This asteroid was one of those rocks, and though wee — measuring somewhere between 16 and 32 feet in diameter — its shockingly close pass by our planet was enough to give astronomers pause.

November 22

When it rains rocks, it pours, or something like that. Unilad reported that an asteroid the size of the Golden Gate Bridge (about 3,280 feet) was heading toward Earth at 56,000 mph. This particular asteroid, identified as 153201 2000 WO107, was first discovered by scientists in New Mexico on November 29, 2000, and they have been tracking it ever since. The big rock was expected to fly past Earth on Sunday, November 29. It was classified as a Near Earth Asteroid (NEA), as it would come within 1.3 astronomical miles of Earth, as well as a Potentially Hazardous Asteroid (PHA).

Meanwhile, down here on solid ground, the southern half of the United States was again in the bullseye for severe storms, said AccuWeather, just as folks were making preparations to celebrate Thanksgiving and feast safely despite growing coronavirus concerns. AccuWeather forecast a multi-faceted storm, "delivering a taste of winter to parts of the Rockies, Plains and Great Lakes" while also punching parts of the South in the form of thunderstorms.

AccuWeather Senior Meteorologist Danny Pydynowski shared, "Damaging wind gusts will be the greatest threat from these storms. However, as storms develop initially, there could be some hail, as well, with the strongest storms, mainly in southeast Kansas, Oklahoma and northeast Texas." He added that tornadoes could not be ruled out either, with the set of weather ingredients expected to take shape.

November 25

Son of a gun. Zombie mink. Oh, 2020, you rascal. To Denmark's horror, the thousands of mink they had slaughtered and buried across the country in shallow pits, over fears of a coronavirus mutation, were rising from the dead, according to The Guardian. "As the bodies decay, gases can be formed," Thomas Kristensen, a national police spokesman, detailed. "This causes the whole thing to expand a little. In this way, in the worst cases, the mink get pushed out of the ground."

Police in West Jutland, where several thousand mink were buried in a mass grave on a military training field, had tried to counter the macabre phenomenon by shoveling extra soil on top of the corpses, which were in a three-foot deep trench.

"This is a natural process," Kristensen said. "Unfortunately, one meter of soil is not just one meter of soil — it depends on what type of soil it is. The problem is that the sandy soil in West Jutland is too light. So we have had to lay more soil on top."

Adding to the much-discussed concern, local media reported that the animals may also have been buried too close to lakes and underground water reserves, prompting fears of possible contamination of ground and drinking water supplies.

November 27

Dozens of bizarre, blue poisonous sea creatures were discovered washed up on a beach in South Africa, stunning locals, reported the New York Post. Shell-less mollusks known as Blue Dragons — the most beautiful killer in the ocean — were found in the sand near Cape Town by a local grandmother.

Maria Wagener said she was strolling on the coast when she spotted more than 20 of the Smurf-like sea slugs, which look like a cross between a lizard, an octopus and a bird. "I probably would have put them back in the sea if I'd had something to lift them — but no, I didn't touch them!" she said. "I pick up starfish all the time and put them back into the sea but I had a feeling that these would have a sting."

Blue Dragons feed on deadly Portuguese man o' war and other venomous aquatic critters, then process their victims' cells to zap predators with an even stronger sting, which can cause nausea, pain and vomiting.

November 30

CNN invited the public to "take a break from online holiday shopping to enjoy the full moon and a penumbral lunar eclipse." This type of eclipse would be possible as the Moon was going to move into the Earth's penumbra, or outer shadow. This had the effect of making the Moon look darker than normal. This was to be the last penumbral eclipse of the year, and would be visible to people in North and South America, Australia, and parts of Asia.

About 85% of the Moon was expected to turn a shade darker during the peak or middle phase of the eclipse. NASA advised that the best chance to see it would likely be through a telescope.

The full moon itself was labeled the Beaver Moon, suggested by Native Americans because they associated it with the period when beavers finished building their lodges to prepare for winter. It was also known as the Frost Moon, due to the cold temperatures of November.

December 2

AccuWeather wasn't talking about an Allstate commercial when they mentioned that "mischief and mayhem" was brewing, as the potential for another big storm in the East became apparent. The first day of meteorological winter, which began on Dec. 1, ushered in the first taste of the season to come with a major lake-effect snowstorm around the Great Lakes and in a few areas of the Northeast, creating travel troubles and power outages. On its heels, forecasters were already eyeing the potential for yet another big storm in the eastern United States.

The storm was expected to strengthen and tap into moisture and just enough cold air to bring drenching rain to many areas, but also the potential for a heavy snowfall in some locations as well. "We have the potential for another snowstorm," AccuWeather Chief Broadcast Meteorologist Bernie Rayno said.

The key as to whether a snowstorm would take shape (versus more widespread rain) was going to be the timing of that storm as it headed into the eastern U.S. If the storm ran out ahead of cold air expected to pour southward from Canada, then it could become a stronger storm and one that unleashed more widespread snow, Rayno said.

Should the storm come to full fruition, it would be the second major storm to hit the eastern U.S. in less than a week. This time, the threat of heavy snow was likely to swing east of areas buried by recent snowfall in the Midwest and lower Great Lakes regions.

December 3

A small earthquake rattled parts of… wait for it… New Jersey and Pennsylvania… according to WCBS NewsRadio 880. The quake, measuring 2.1 in magnitude, according to the U.S. Geological Survey, was felt in parts of northwestern New Jersey and eastern Pennsylvania. No damage or injuries were reported.

The quake's center was Milford, New Jersey, the same area where a smaller quake (1.7 magnitude) had occurred on Aug. 19.

December 4

As unlikely as the NJ/PA quake, was a meteor exploding over New York, from which people actually felt the shockwave, according to BGR.

"2020 has been a rough year for pretty much the entire world. Lots of people have joked that they wish a giant meteor would just slam into Earth and 'get it over with'," said BGR. The lesson was "Be careful what you wish for."

A space rock speeding through the solar system lined up perfectly with Earth, slamming into our planet's atmosphere and causing a large boom. According to Syracuse.com, the rock sent a shockwave that was felt for miles, causing windows to shake and even tripping earthquake detectors in the area. Nearly 200 reports were filed with the American Meteor Society by individuals who either saw or heard it. Those reports were detailed enough for scientists to figure out what had happened. Debris from the object reportedly rained down over a wide area, though the vast majority of it was almost certainly incinerated due to the intense friction.

December 7

There was something really fishy about a lake catch in South Carolina, the New York Post related. A specialist hired by Greenville County Recreation discovered a nine-pound goldfish in Oak Grove Lake. "Anyone missing their goldfish?" the rec dept. posted to Twitter, included with a photo of the monster goldfish.

The goldfish was recovered while the specialist was electrofishing, a method that stuns the fish and causes them to float to the surface. Electrofishing does not harm the water dwelling creatures and the goldfish was released back into the lake as it did not pose a threat to the ecosystem, the department said.

Up in Minnesota, meanwhile, hoar frost had created a winter wonderland, reported AccuWeather. Trees in Graceville were muffled in the strange coating, creating a stunning wintry scene. Hoar frost is named after its hair-like appearance. The size of the frost that forms depends on how much water vapor is available to "feed" the ice crystals as they grow.

There was *another* hairy situation occurring in an Australian suburb, according to AccuWeather. An intense windstorm left parts of Hillside, outside of Melbourne, buried under an overabundance of tumbleweed. The bizarre weather event had residents in stunned amazement at the sheer volume of the grasses that blew in — some piled waist-deep. The tumbleweeds covered streets, yards and a pool and even piled up in front of people's front doors, preventing them from using their entryways. One man was seen trying to clean up the mass amounts of tumbleweed from his property, which appeared to be an exercise in futility given that the garbage can he was using was completely overflowing with the brown grass.

AccuWeather Broadcast Meteorologist Adam Del Rosso called the deposit "freakish". Margaret Prosaic, a local resident, described it as a "grass storm", adding, "And it's just completely taken over our back yard, and front yard." Another resident, Naomi Gauci, contributed, "Not in the 15 years we've been here, have we ever seen this sort of thing happen."

Known as "hairy panic" or "witch grass", the tumbleweeds blew in seemingly out of nowhere, according to residents. Local reports suggested the grasses may have blown in from a horse paddock located nearby.

December 8

What a whale of a sighting: a humpback whale, to be clear, spotted swimming in the Hudson River near midtown Manhattan, according to WCBS NewsRadio 880. Twitter user Andres Javier recorded video of the massive mammal breaching the surface near Pier 84. The clip showed the whale was near the Intrepid Sea, Air and Space Museum. Footage showed the whale shooting water from its blowhole before heading back into the water. Experts suggested that the whale was drawn to the area by an abundance of food.

The only other time in recent memory a big mammal like this was in the area was in 2016, when another humpback whale took up residency in the Hudson River for about a week. The river has an abundance of Menhaden, commonly called "bunker", that the whale prefers.

December 9

Crystal clear ice had formed for miles along Sea Gull Lake in northern Minnesota, reported WCCO-TV, Minnesota.

"This year was super rare. I know some of my friends who have lived here for 25 years have never seen it like this," Cassidy Ritter, of Voyager Canoe Outfitters, said. "It was breathtaking. I couldn't believe I was ice skating in the Boundary Waters. It was the most amazing feeling ever. Magical, and the sunset and the snow in the trees. It was just absolutely beautiful," Ritter said. His brother, Matt, added, "It was clear and there wasn't even snow on the ice, nothing. It was quite eerie. Even the dogs were unsure of it because they could see through it," Matt Ritter said.

And as the ice was forming on Minnesota waters, the sun… yes, the sun.. was launching an explosion of electromagnetic energy towards Earth, said CNN, forcing the issuance of a Geomagnetic Storm Watch. The burst had the potential of creating a spectacular display of the Northern Lights as far south as Pennsylvania and Oregon. Communication disruptions were possible, though, too.

CNN termed the explosion a "massive solar belch", propelling highly charged coronal matter across the solar system.

December 10

The sun's belch created the possibility that we *Connecticut* folks could get the rare chance to see the Northern Lights, too, if clouds didn't get in the way, according to NBC CT.

The National Weather Service in Cleveland, Ohio, said the unique situation was creating a buzz on social media. The service shared a map showing locations where the Northern Lights might be visible, which included our Nutmeg State on the southern cusp of possible visibility.

One thing folks were *more* likely to see, at least more south, was freezing fog. AccuWeather said the National Weather Service in Mount Holly, New Jersey, located about 20 miles east of Philadelphia, issued a freezing fog advisory for a portion of southeastern Pennsylvania and much of New Jersey.

The seldom-used advisory was met with befuddlement from a few social media users. "Is this just frost or is 2020 now affecting the weather, too?" asked one of the users. The NWS replied, though, that the condition was not a new one. "It's just a bit *rarer* here rather than across the Midwest," it explained.

Freezing fog is fog that forms when the temperature at the surface is at or below the freezing mark (32F).

"In addition to the hazard of reduced visibility that comes with fog, freezing fog brings additional dangers," AccuWeather Meteorologist Ryan Adamson said. "When freezing fog forms, any moisture deposited by the fog onto roadways can also freeze. This can cause icy spots, especially on bridges and overpasses, so motorists need to exercise extra caution when there is fog with temperatures below freezing."

Untreated sidewalks could also develop a slippery glaze of ice during freezing fog events, putting unsuspecting pedestrians at risk for falls. At airports, freezing fog events can lead to flight delays due to deicing operations and even cancellations. If the freezing fog is very thick and/or persists for several hours or even days, ice can accumulate on trees, bushes, signs, power lines and other exposed surfaces. "While the ice can look very pretty, the extra weight of the ice on trees and power lines can cause them to come down, which can lead to power outages," Adamson said.

December 13

Remember that humpback whale in the Hudson and its hunger for bunker? Well, masses of the ubiquitous menhaden had been washing up all along *Connecticut's* shore, too – as well as from New Jersey to Cape Cod – over the past month, according to the CT Examiner. To beach strollers, the sightings were alarming, but biologists said the dead fish weren't a cause for alarm. The number of bunker washing up was just a *small percentage* of the bunker that were still swimming in Long Island Sound, explained Bill Lucey, of Save the Sound.

Bunker spawn in the Chesapeake in February and March, make their way north to the Gulf of Maine in the spring, then head back down south as the water gets colder in the fall, according to Lacey. This year, higher than usual numbers of the fish congregated in the Sound, and they missed their cue to start heading south because the water in the Sound stayed warm into the fall. As the water temperature dropped in October and November, the supply of algae and plankton for bunker to eat diminished, leaving the fish hungry and cold and causing a small percentage to die and wash ashore.

December 14

This was our kind of entertainment: NASA was going to live stream the total solar eclipse! The celestial event — when the moon blocks the sun and creates temporary darkness along the path of totality — was only going to be visible from the ground across the southern end of South America. So, NASA stepped up through a partnership with Pontificia Universidad Católica de Chile via telescopes at the Observatorio Docente. The only caveat to NASA's total solar eclipse coverage was that it would only be in Spanish.

December 16

We here in southwestern CT were busy gazing at something else — a forecast of an impending 12-18 inches of snow, falling at a rate of up to two inches per hour. Our Fairfield First Selectwoman Brenda Kupchick shared in an alert that there could "be some minor coastal flooding and wind gusts that could lead to power outages" and that our Public Works and Emergency Responders were prepared. FS Kupchick warned, "In light of the expected whiteout conditions and limited visibility, I urge residents to stay off the roads and to not park on the streets to allow DPW to plow safely. If you must travel, please exercise extreme caution."

Remarkably, the predicted snow wouldn't necessarily interrupt schooling as it had in the past, according to NBC CT. With all the remote learning schoolchildren had gotten used to during the pandemic, that same type of teaching could effectively be facilitated on school days that might otherwise be canceled due to snow.

"Growing up in Connecticut, kids have always associated winter with snow days — a surprise reprieve from school, filled with sledding and other frozen fun. So, normally in weeks like this, children around the state would be getting excited," NBC CT shared. "But this is not a normal year… and that excitement has been tempered. When it comes to inclement weather, school districts now have a choice. They can decide between remote learning or use a traditional 'snow day.'"

Waterbury was one of several districts that had decided to continue distance learning. "With the pandemic and opportunities that our students and staff have now with virtual learning, we decided not to discredit an opportunity for a day of learning," said Waterbury Superintendent of Schools Dr. Verna Ruffin. Waterbury said the only exception to its inclement weather policy would be if there was a widespread power outage preventing students from logging on. Otherwise it was going to be business as usual.

On the other side of the world, Fiji was facing a much scarier weather challenge, according to the Washington Post. Tropical Cyclone Yasa, the strongest storm on Earth at the time of this report, was headed for a potentially devastating landfall in that country within the next 24 hours. The storm was packing sustained winds estimated at 160 miles per hour, which made it the equivalent of a Category 5 storm. It threatened to cause damage on the scale of Tropical Cyclone Winston, which caused widespread destruction when it hit the country in 2016.

December 17

The forecasted snow in the Northeast was no joke. Not only did it appear, it did its worst, dropping more snow in parts of the region than all of last year's winter season, according to CNN. Winter Storm Gail, as it was named, delivered heavy snow across the Northeast, blanketing much of Pennsylvania, New York and New England, and creating slick road conditions across the region. People living in and around New York City, Philadelphia and Boston received generally between six to 12 inches of snow. New York's Central Park saw 10.5 inches, more than what fell during last year's entire paltry winter season, the National Weather Service noted.

Parts of central Pennsylvania and upstate New York received the brunt of the snowfall, according to the NWS. New York Gov. Andrew Cuomo declared a state of emergency for 18 counties due to the snowstorm. He said there were 600 car accidents and two storm-related deaths.

Wellsboro, Pennsylvania, got a whopping 18.8 inches of snow, while Albany, New York, was hit with over 22 inches. The NWS office in Binghamton, New York, tallied nearly 40 inches of snow, their largest total since records began in 1951. That made it Binghamton's heaviest snowstorm on record, topping the previous record of 35.3 inches set during Winter Storm Stella on March 14-15, 2017.

Weather.com added that Binghamton averages 81.8 inches of snow each winter season. This winter storm produced roughly half that seasonal average in less than 24 hours.

It was also possible the winter storm might have set new 24-hour snowfall records in two states: Vermont and Pennsylvania. A preliminary storm total of 44.8 inches was measured in southern Vermont near Peru. That total would top Vermont's all-time state 24-hour snowfall record (42 inches at Jay Peak on Feb. 5, 1995), according to NOAA. Pennsylvania's top snow total was 43.3 inches near Alba in the north-central part of the state, easily bypassing the state's current record for most snowfall in 24 hours, at 38 inches.

Out west, meanwhile, Vegas was crushing a record dry streak, according to Weather.com. McCarran International Airport, the city's official reporting station, did not observe measurable rain (0.01 inches or greater) for 240 consecutive days in 2020. The dry stretch began April

20 and finally ended Dec. 17. That easily beat the previous record streak without measurable rain in Las Vegas of 150 days set from Feb. 22 to July 21, 1959, according to the NWS.

Part of the reason for this long stretch of dryness, said experts, was that the summertime monsoon brought very little rainfall in the Southwest in 2020. Of the minuscule number of showers and thunderstorms it produced, none of this activity dropped anything more than a trace of rain on Las Vegas.

December 19

Snake-infested sea foam, oh boy! That's what the Matador Network reported for Eastern Australia. "It looks like something out of an otherworldly apocalyptic movie, but in reality, it's just a little sea foam. To be fair, it's more like an *onslaught* of sea foam, whipped up by intense storms this week that's covering the beaches of New South Wales and Queensland, Australia. While you might be tempted to flop right into it like diving into fluffy snow, you should probably think twice because sea snakes and other materials are lurking under the soft surface. Yes, you might be jumping into snake-infested sea foam," the network shared.

Although people were certainly enjoying the foam — both playing in it and taking photos of it — officials were advising to steer clear due to the presence of the aforementioned sea snakes, which could have gotten swept up in the foam. There are 32 species of poisonous sea snakes around the country, and their bites require anti-venom.

The stormy waters were also bringing large debris to the shore, said Nathan Fife, the Gold Coast lifesaving services supervisor at Surf Lifesaving Australia. "There have been trees and things like that have washed up. I think there was half a cow that washed up at the beach yesterday, so make sure of what's in front of you. There are trees and logs floating around, so please be careful," he cautioned.

Poof. That was the sound of a black hole vanishing that was up to 100 billion times the mass of the sun. Said Digital Trends, "You'd think that it would be hard to lose one of the largest black holes in the universe. However, scientists are currently puzzled by the apparent absence of the supermassive black hole at the center of the Abell 2261 galaxy cluster — a monster that is estimated to be somewhere between three billion and 100 billion times the mass of the sun," DT shared.

At the center of almost every galaxy, including our own, is a supermassive black hole. These black holes usually scale with the size of the galaxy, so the bigger the galaxy, the bigger the black hole. Abell 2261, located 2.7 billion light years away, has a very large central galaxy and so it *should* have a similarly large supermassive black hole. But, strangely, astronomers had been unable to locate this particular black hole anywhere, DT explained.

Data from over the years produced by a variety of instruments — including the Subaru Telescope, the Hubble Space Telescope, and the Chandra X-Ray Observatory — was examined. In combing through the Chandra data, in particular, scientists looked for evidence that the black hole had somehow been ejected from its position at the galaxy's center. While the study didn't find any evidence of the black hole itself, it did find some suggestions that a *merger* may have taken place.

A merger, DT shared, is a dramatic event when two galaxies merge and the central black holes of each galaxy also merge, throwing out ripples called gravitational waves. If these waves are not evenly distributed in all directions, the black hole could be set zipping off away from its place at the heart of the galaxy. This suggestion, called a "recoiling black hole", is only theoretical, as such a thing has never been observed before. But if true, it could provide an exciting new way for scientists to study gravitational waves.

December 21

Skywatchers looking to the stars above were in for a special treat, said People – and no, it was not an early peek at Santa's sleigh. A planetary conjunction between Saturn and Jupiter was set to take place on the winter solstice. Its proximity to the holidays had earned it the nickname "Christmas Star."

Planets appearing to pass each other in the solar system is a regular occurrence, and Jupiter and Saturn are aligned in the sky about once every 20 years, according to NASA. But this year, they were going to be passing closer than they had in nearly 400 years, and just a tenth of a degree apart. And, for the first time in nearly 800 years, their alignment was going to happen at night.

December 22

CNN told us Earth dwellers to keep our eyes turned to the heavens for another sighting as well: the oft-ignored Ursid meteor shower, on the heels of the winter solstice. The small meteor shower could only been seen from the Northern Hemisphere, with between five and 10 meteors streaking across the sky per hour.

Meanwhile, Earth residents, particularly those in the western U.S., were also being cautioned about avalanches after three people were killed by them in Colorado, according to NBC. A rescue team recovered the bodies of skiers caught in an avalanche near Ophir Pass in southwestern Colorado's San Juan Mountains, the San Juan County Office of Emergency Management said. Colorado's snowpack was the weakest it had been since 2012, triggering 132 recent avalanches in the state.

December 24

We here in southwestern Connecticut were expecting *Santa* to come to town this Eve — *not* a bout of severe weather. Our Fairfield, CT First Selectwoman Brenda Kupchick shared that "forecasts predict that very heavy rain and strong winds are likely to cause flooding conditions and power outages. Homes that are prone to basement flooding should take precautions as the heavy rains and rapid snowmelt can cause flooding. Scattered power outages are likely. Please plan ahead by keeping thermostats up overnight. Our Emergency Management Team is prepared to work with UI to resolve issues as quickly as possible."

Fairfield HamletHub elevated the urgency of the weather condition, when the NWS later issued a SEVERE STORM WARNING. The expectation was for "2-4 inches of rain, flooding in low areas, wind gusts of up to 55mph, tree damage, actual downed trees, and likely power outages."

Weather watchers advised staying indoors, and away from windows due to flying debris. Locals were also encouraged to secure or put safely away anything loose on their properties and to stay tuned for official bulletins.

December 27

The U.K. was also getting buffeted, by hurricane-force winds, said the Independent. Storm Bella blew into England and Wales triggering weather warnings across much of Britain. Gusts of more than 100mph were recorded on the Isle of Wight and several people in Yorkshire had to be rescued by emergency services after they were left stranded in their flooded cars.

The storm brought disruption on roads and railways, while amber warnings from the Met Office remained in force as the storm continued to pass across the country. A gust of 83mph was recorded at Aberdaron in north Wales, according to the Met Office. Gusts reached 79mph on the Isle of Portland in Dorset and 74mph in Mount Batten, near Plymouth, Devon. The Needles Coastwatch Station on the Isle of Wight recorded gusting winds of 106mph. "Were Bella a tropical storm, it would now be a Category 2 hurricane according to the Saffir-Simpson scale," Met tweeted.

December 29

2020 was giving it its all. REUTERS reported that a quake had struck Croatia and Slovenia, killing a child, injuring many and damaging structures. The magnitude 6.4 quake was centered in Petrinja, 30 miles south of Zagreb in central Croatia. Rescuers tried to pull people from the rubble of collapsed buildings, television footage showed, and army troops were sent into the area to help. Tomislav Fabijanic, head of emergency medical services in nearby Sisak, said many people had been injured in Petrinja and Sisak.

Overhead, a full cold moon was set to illuminate the heavens, kicking off Winter's astronomical calendar, days before the quadranids meteor shower was set to streak across the sky, said Newsweek. The Cold Moon would be the 13th and final full moon of 2020, and also the highest in the night sky as viewed from Earth.

The assignation derived from the Mohawk Native Americans of the northeastern area of what is now New York State, southern Canada and Vermont. They used the term to mark the chilly temperatures that characterize the winter season.

Names of a similar vein are used by the Cree, who traditionally call it the Hoar Frost Moon; the Haida and Cherokee, who name it the Snow Moon; the Western Abenaki, who call it the Winter Maker Moon; and the Mohicans, who term it the Long Night Moon, according to the Old Farmers Almanac. In some parts of Europe it is traditionally known as the Moon After Yule.

December 30

This second to last day of the year provided a summit to look back at 2020 and sum up all the unbelievable, record-shattering weather, space and animal-oriented occurrences. In no particular order, then:

Hottest Year on Record?

According to NASA, Earth's average surface temperature in 2020 was likely to tie with 2016 for the hottest year on record, making the last seven years the seven hottest on record, relayed EcoWatch. Remarkably, the record warmth of 2020 occurred during a minimum in the solar cycle and in a year in which a moderate La Niña event formed. Surface cooling of the tropical Pacific during La Niña events typically causes a slight global cool-down, as does the minimum of the solar cycle, making it difficult to set all-time heat records. The record heat of 2020 in these circumstances suggested human-driven emissions might be influencing global warming.

The Wild 2020 Atlantic Hurricane Season

The 2020 Atlantic hurricane season produced an extraordinary 30 named storms (highest on record), 13 hurricanes (second-highest on record) and six major hurricanes (tied for second-highest on record), more than double the activity of an average season (12 named storms, 6 hurricanes, and 3 major hurricanes), according to EcoWatch.

The 2020 season was notable not only for its record number of named storms (after breaking into the Greek alphabet by the ridiculously early date of September 18), but also for its record number of rapidly intensifying storms (10), record number of landfalling U.S. named storms (12), and record number of landfalling U.S. hurricanes (six). Every single mile of the mainland U.S. coast from Texas to Maine was under a watch or warning related to tropical cyclones at some point in 2020. U.S. hurricane damage exceeded $37 billion, according to insurance broker Aon, the eighth-highest annual total on record, said EcoWatch.

Two catastrophic Category 4 hurricanes hit Central America in November: Hurricane Iota, the latest category 5 storm ever recorded in the Atlantic, and Hurricane Eta, the deadliest tropical cyclone worldwide in 2020, with at least 274 people listed as dead or missing. At least seven hurricanes from 2020 would be worthy of having their names retired: Iota, Eta, Zeta, Delta, Sally, Laura, and Isaias – although there is still no official mechanism for retiring storm names from the Greek alphabet. The record for most names retired in one Atlantic season was set in 2005, when five hurricanes had their names retired, EcoWatch summarized.

High Atmospheric Carbon Dioxide Levels Despite Record Emissions Drop

As a result of restrictions taken to curb the coronavirus pandemic, carbon emissions to the atmosphere in 2020 declined by nine to 10% in the U.S. and six to seven percent globally, although some of those reductions were offset by carbon released by wildfires. Those were the largest annual carbon emissions declines since World War II and far more than the one percent global and six percent U.S. emissions drops brought about by the 2008 Great Recession, said EcoWatch.

Nevertheless, atmospheric carbon dioxide levels rose by 2.6 parts per million from 2019 to 414 ppm in 2020. The amount of carbon in the atmosphere, suggested EcoWatch, will not decline until human emissions reach net zero. Moreover, as coronavirus restrictions were lifted during 2020, global carbon pollution nearly rebounded to pre-COVID levels.

An Apocalyptic Wildfire Season

The year 2020 brought record levels of fire activity to the U.S. and Arctic, but unusually low levels in Canada and tropical Africa, resulting in a below-average year for global fire activity, according to the Copernicus Atmosphere Monitoring Service, as relayed by EcoWatch.

According to Insurance broker Aon, the global direct cost of wildfires in 2020 was $17 billion, ranking as the fifth-costliest wildfire year, behind 2017, 2018, 2015 (major Indonesian fires), and 2010 (major Russian fires).

The Australian bushfire season ending in early 2020 (due to seasons in the Southern hemisphere being the reverse of those in the Northern hemisphere) was also a record-breaker, having burned more than 46 million acres and destroyed more than 3,500 homes, said EcoWatch.

The National Interagency Fire Center reported that U.S. wildfires burned 10.25 million acres as of December 18, 2020, the highest yearly total since accurate records began in 1983. The previous record was 10.13 million acres in 2015. The hottest August through October period in Western U.S. history, combined with severe drought and a once-in-a-generation offshore wind event, conspired to bring about an apocalyptic western U.S. wildfire season. Total U.S. wildfire damages in 2020 were $16.5 billion, said Aon, ranking as the third-costliest year on record, behind 2017 ($24 billion) and 2018 ($22 billion). Wildfires caused at least 43 direct U.S. deaths. But the indirect death toll among people 65 and older in California alone during the period August 1 to September 10 – due to wildfire smoke inhalation – was likely between 1,200 and 3,000, researchers at Stanford University reported in a September 11 study. The 4.2 million acres burned in California in 2020 was more than double the previous record set in 2018.

Most Expensive 2020 Disaster: China Flooding Causes $32B in Damage

Seasonal monsoon flooding in China in June through September killed 278 people, damaged or destroyed 1.4 million homes and businesses, and did $32 billion in damage, according to insurance broker Aon, as relayed by EcoWatch. EM-DAT, the international disaster database, ranks that total as the third-most expensive non-U.S. weather disaster since accurate records began in 1990 (adjusted for inflation), behind 1998 flooding in China ($48 billion) and 2011 flooding in Thailand ($47 billion).

In a September 2020 study published in the Bulletin of the American Meteorological Society, "Each 0.5 degrees Celsius of Warming Increases Annual Flood Losses in China by More than US $60 Billion", researchers found that annual average flood losses in China during the period 1984-2018 were $19.2 billion (2015 dollars), which was 0.5% of China's GDP. Annual flood losses increased to $25.3 billion annually during the period 2006-2018. The study authors predicted that each additional 0.5 degrees Celsius of global warming would increase China flood losses by $60 billion per year.

A Near-Record Number of Global Billion-Dollar Weather Disasters

Through the end of November, 44 billion-dollar weather disasters had occurred globally in 2020, according to the November 2020 Catastrophe Report from insurance broker Aon, relayed by EcoWatch. The record in the Aon database is 47, set in 2010, and 2020 could challenge that record.

The United States suffered 25 billion-dollar weather disasters in 2020, surpassing Aon's previous U.S. record of 20 in 2017. The record number of U.S. disasters led to the American Red Cross providing record levels of disaster sheltering in 2020, according to a December 2 article by E&E News.

Near-Record Low Arctic Sea Ice

Arctic sea ice reached its annual minimum on September 15, 2020, bottoming out at its second-lowest extent and volume ever recorded, behind 2012, said Yale Climate Connections. A new study suggested that the 2012 record hadn't been broken despite ever-rising temperatures because the rapidly-warming Arctic has altered the jet stream, leading to cloudy summer Arctic conditions that have acted to temporarily preserve some of the sea ice. However, long-term global warming was expected to inevitably win out, and scientists expected the Arctic to be ice-free in the summer beginning sometime between 2030 and 2050. Overall, three-quarters of the volume of summer sea ice in the Arctic had melted over the past 40 years.

Northeast Snow Took a Vacation

As far as snow was concerned, you could say parts of the East really didn't have much of a winter season in 2019-20, according to Weather.com. Neither Philadelphia nor Washington D.C. could scrape up a measly inch of snow the entire season. Only the 1972-73 season was less snowy in Philadelphia than 2019-20 (Philadelphia averages about 22 inches of snow each season). "The overall winter pattern set up for many 'Colorado low alley' type winter storms," winter weather expert Tom Niziol told Weather.com, referring to a storm track northeastward from the High Plains of eastern Colorado into the Plains. If a nor'easter did form, it either was too far offshore and moved away quickly or lacked cold air. Most often, low pressure tracked well inland, instead of offshore, pumping warmer air into the East and taking snow off the table, particularly along the Interstate 95 urban corridor.

December 31

The ultimate farewell to 2020? An epic space cloud offering a good riddance, reported by Science Alert. "Sometimes, the Universe provides just the perfect method for expressing our feelings. A space cloud 7,500 light years away has given us the most appropriate farewell we can think of for this whole dumpster fire of a year, 2020. This small clump of material is part of a much larger cloud complex called the Carina Nebula, and under normal circumstances would not be given a nickname of its own. But its distinctive shape — fist-like with an upraised middle finger — has led scientists to nickname it the Defiant Finger," SA shared.

And that's exactly what it looked like: the age-old obscene gesture translating to "go do ghastly things to yourself" and "go away", but in much ruder words.

Printed in the United States
by Baker & Taylor Publisher Services